ESTHER

Discover Together Bible Study Series

1 Peter: Discovering Encouragement in Troubling Times
1 Timothy: Discovering Clarity in a World That Can't Agree
1 and 2 Thessalonians: Discovering Hope in a Promised Future
Daniel: Discovering the Courage to Stand for Your Faith
Ecclesiastes: Discovering Meaning in a Meaningless World
Ephesians: Discovering Your Identity and Purpose in Christ
Esther: Discovering God's Enduring Care for His People
Galatians: Discovering Freedom in Christ Through Daily Practice
Hebrews: Discovering a Better Fulfillment in Jesus
Hosea: Discovering God's Fierce Love
Isaiah: Discovering Assurance Through Prophecies About Your Mighty King
James: Discovering the Joy of Living Out Your Faith
Luke: Discovering Healing in Jesus's Words to Women
Philippians: Discovering Joy Through Relationship
Proverbs: Discovering Ancient Wisdom for a Postmodern World, Volume 1
Proverbs: Discovering Ancient Wisdom for a Postmodern World, Volume 2
Psalms: Discovering Authentic Worship
Revelation: Discovering Life for Today and Eternity
Ruth: Discovering God's Faithfulness in an Anxious World

Leader's guides are available at www.discovertogetherseries.com.

ESTHER

Discovering God's Enduring Care for His People

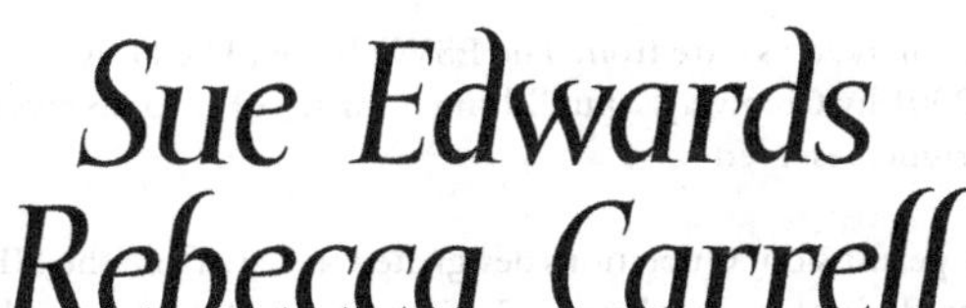

Esther: Discovering God's Enduring Care for His People

Published by Kregel Publications, a division of Kregel Inc., 2450 Oak Industrial Dr. NE, Grand Rapids, MI 49505. www.kregel.com.

With gratitude to Dr. Edwards's interns Jenica McMaster and Cynthia Fowler.

Cataloging-in-Publication data is available from the Library of Congress.

ISBN 978-0-8254-4938-3

Printed in the United States of America
26 27 28 29 30 31 32 33 34 35 / 5 4 3 2 1

Contents

Why Study the Bible?

Varied voices perpetually shout for our attention. Who should we listen to? Who can we believe? The Uber driver we've never met but count on to take us home? The man hawking cell phones behind the counter? The woman on the treadmill beside us? Maybe we can trust them; maybe we can't. Over time we can discern whether or not we're comfortable inviting them into our personal space or giving weight to their opinions. But the reality is that, ultimately, everyone will disappoint us, and we will disappoint them too.

Only God is perfectly trustworthy. Only God offers a way to combat the chaos rocking our world right now. Only God sent us a Love Letter that leads to peace and stability despite the turmoil that surrounds us. "All Scripture is God-breathed and is useful for teaching, rebuking, correcting and training in righteousness, so that the servant of God may be thoroughly equipped for every good work" (2 Timothy 3:16–17).

Years ago a wise woman, who secretly paid for my (Sue's) daughters to attend a Christian school we couldn't afford, planted that truth in my mind and heart. This concept blossomed into realistic expectations and a hearty hunger for a relationship with that perfectly trustworthy one. That hunger led to a lifetime of savoring God's Love Letter, the Scriptures, and that relationship and practice upended everything. Wherever you are in your journey, Jesus invites you to experience the contentment and peace that only he can provide, regardless of your circumstances.

Jesus promised, "Peace I leave with you; my peace I give you. I do not give to you as the world gives. Do not let your hearts be troubled and do not be afraid" (John 14:27). The book of Esther pictures the sovereignty of God amid trials of every kind. Trials that we still face today, although they may look different in our cultural context. Submerge yourself with us in the book of Esther so that together we can be encouraged that God, the trustworthy one, will be faithful in our trials and chaos, just as he has been for every generation.

How to Get the Most out of a Discover Together Bible Study

We're all at different junctures in our spiritual migrations, but God's Word doesn't separate us according to superficial differences. We all want to know God intimately and flourish, and we can all learn from one another. "As iron sharpens iron, so one person sharpens another" (Proverbs 27:17).

Discover Together Bible Studies are designed to promote unity, for all women to learn from and enjoy together regardless of age, stage, race, nationality, spiritual maturity, or economic or educational status. God proclaims we are all sisters in his forever family preparing to spend eternity together (Matthew 12:46–50).

However, our schedules vary week to week depending on the needs of loved ones, travel responsibilities, and work demands. To honor these differences, this study provides two choices:

1. Basic questions that require about one and a half hours of prep a week, offering in-depth Bible study with a minimum time commitment.
2. "Digging Deeper" questions for women who want to probe the text more deeply.

Women wanting to tackle the "Digging Deeper" questions may

- need resources such as an atlas, Bible dictionary, or concordance;
- check online resources and compare parallel passages for additional insight;
- use an interlinear Greek-English text or expository dictionary to do word studies;
- grapple with complex theological issues and differing views; and
- create outlines and charts and write essays worthy of seminarians.

In addition to God's Love Letter, we also need authentic community, a place to be ourselves where we are loved unconditionally despite our differences and challenged to grow.

This Bible study is designed for either individual or group discovery, but you will benefit more if you tackle each week's lesson on your own and then meet with other women to share insights, struggles, and aha moments.

If you choose to meet together, someone needs to lead the group. You can find a free downloadable leader's guide for each study, along with tips for facilitating small groups with excellence, at discovertogetherseries.com.

Choose a realistic level of Bible study that fits your schedule. You may want to finish the basic questions first and then dig deeper as time permits. Take time to savor the questions, and don't rush through the application.

Read the sidebars for additional insight to enrich the experience. Note the optional passages to memorize, and determine if this discipline would be helpful for you.

Do not allow yourself to be intimidated by women who have walked with the Lord longer, who have more time, or who are gifted differently. You bring something to the table no one else can contribute.

Prioritize your study. Consider spacing your study throughout the week to allow time to ponder and meditate on what the Holy Spirit is teaching you. Do not make other appointments during the group Bible study. Ask God to enable you to attend faithfully.

Come with an excitement to learn from others and a desire to share yourself and your journey. Give it your best, and you'll find the only one who will never let you down.

WHAT IS AN INDUCTIVE STUDY, AND WHY IS IT SO POWERFUL?

The Discover Together series uses inductive Bible study as a structure to dig into the Bible. *Inductive* means using specific observations to determine general principles. Inductive study is the practice of investigating or interviewing a Bible passage to determine its true meaning, attempting to leave behind any presuppositions or personal agendas.

First, we seek to learn what the original author meant when writing to the original audience. We carefully examine the words and ideas. We ask questions like, What is happening? Who is it happening to? And where is it happening? Only after we answer those questions are we ready to discern what we think God meant.

Once we are clear about what God meant, then we are ready to apply these truths to our present circumstances, trusting that a steady diet of truth will result in an enriched relationship with almighty God and beneficial changes in our character, actions, and attitudes.

Inductive study is powerful because discerning biblical truth is the best way we grow in faith, thrive in our lives, and deepen our relationship with the God who created us.

To experience this powerful process, we must immerse ourselves in the practice of study as a lifestyle—and not just focus on a verse here and there. Our life goal must be to digest the Bible, whole book by whole book, as life-giving nourishment that cannot be attained any other way.

Over a span of sixteen hundred years, God orchestrated the creation of sixty-six biblical documents written by the Holy Spirit through more than forty human authors who came from different backgrounds. Together they produced a unified Love Letter that communicates without error God's affection, grace, direction, truth, and wisdom. He did this so that we would not be left without access to his mind and heart.[1]

THE INCREDIBLE BENEFITS OF BIBLICAL LITERACY

Earning a quality education changes us. It makes us literate and alters our future. Many of us sacrifice years, money, and energy to educate ourselves because we understand education's benefits and rewards.

Biblical literacy is even more valuable than secular education! But just like with secular learning, becoming biblically literate requires serious investment. However, the life-changing rewards and benefits far outweigh a diploma and increased lifetime earnings from the most prestigious Ivy League university.

A few benefits to Bible study include

- a more intimate relationship with almighty God;
- an understanding of the way the world works and how to live well in it;
- a supernatural ability to love ourselves and others;
- insight into our own sin nature along with a path to overcome it, and, when we fail, a way to wipe the shame slate clean, pick ourselves up as forgiven, and move on with renewed hope;
- meaning and purpose;
- relational health experienced in community;
- support through struggles;
- continued growth in becoming a person who exhibits the fruit of the Spirit: love, joy, peace, forbearance, kindness, goodness, faithfulness, gentleness, and self-control (Galatians 5:22–23); and
- contentment as we learn to trust in God's providential care.

Every book of the Bible provides another layer in the scaffolding of truth that transforms our minds, hearts, attitudes, and actions. What truths wait to be unearthed in the book of Esther, and how will they change us?

Why Study Esther?

A couple of years ago, I (Rebecca) noticed a lump growing on my dog's side. Concerned, I took her to the vet, who reassured me that it was a fatty lipoma—not much to look at but perfectly harmless. Today, my sweet pooch is covered in lumps. Literally. While each protrusion is a part of my dog, it's a nonfunctioning part. It's a spare appendage off to the side that plays no vital role. We could remove it and never miss it.

Through the centuries, many Christians have treated Esther much the same way—as though the book is a *part* of the Bible, but a nonfunctioning part. Like a weird appendage buried in the Old Testament that plays no vital role and that we could remove and never miss. In fact, Martin Luther reportedly hated it and wanted it excised from the canon of Scripture, claiming it had "too many heathen unnaturalities."[1] At first blush, one could understand why. Several features (or the absence thereof) set Esther apart from the rest of the Old Testament.

First, the author never mentions God. Not once, in any form or by any name. Nor does he mention prayer, the temple, miracles, or the Levitical law.

Second, the events take place well outside the land God promised to Abraham, Isaac, and Jacob. The story unfolds in Susa, the capital city of Persia. Curious, indeed, because the Persian rulers Cyrus and Darius had previously decreed that the Jews could go back to Jerusalem to rebuild the city's walls and the temple. But some Jews, including Mordecai and Esther, the story's key players, chose not to return.

Third, unlike Deuteronomy, Isaiah, or Psalms, which are heavily quoted by early Jewish and Christian writers, Esther receives relatively little attention in these later sources. None of the New Testament authors mention the book of Esther, and it is the only Old Testament work not found among the Dead Sea Scrolls, which contain our oldest known copies of all the others.

Other Christians have complained that Esther's story contributes little to the narrative arc of the Bible. No prophecies about the Messiah. No mention of a coming kingdom. No hint or hope of the day of the Lord. Some over the centuries have wondered: Was Esther's inclusion in the biblical canon an accident? Is Esther merely bonus material? Or might the author be up to something? Could the absence of any mention of God convey a message in itself? What if this little appendage of a book, so often neglected, preaches the gospel at top volume to those willing to listen?

That, dear friend, is what we shall endeavor to find out. For if "all Scripture is God-breathed and is useful for teaching, rebuking, correcting and training in righteousness" (2 Timothy 3:16), then Esther contains treasure waiting to be unearthed.

ESTHER'S CONTRIBUTION TO THE BIBLE

We find Esther in the Old Testament at the end of the section scholars refer to as *historical narrative*. In other words, Esther caps off the portion of Scripture that tells the story of the birth, rise, fall, and partial redemption of Israel.

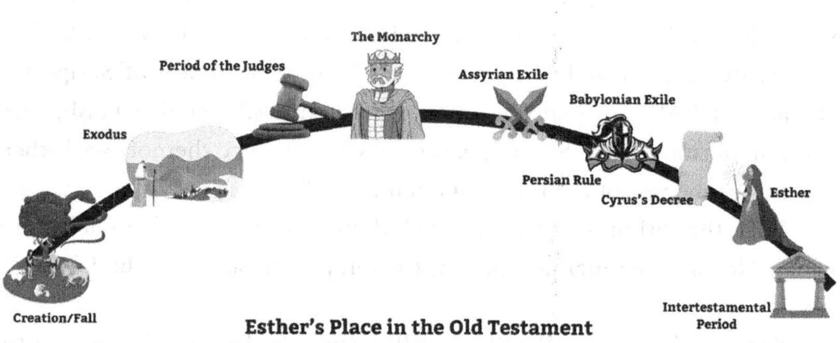

Esther's Place in the Old Testament

To summarize briefly, in Genesis, God promised land, offspring, and a blessing to Abraham. In Exodus, God chose Moses to deliver his people out of Egypt, through the Red Sea, and to the base of Mount Sinai to receive the Ten Commandments and instructions for the tabernacle. However, the people failed to obey God after their liberation, so instead of moving directly into the promised land, the Hebrews wandered in the wilderness for approximately forty years. During this period, Moses wrote the first five books of the Old Testament (Genesis–Deuteronomy).

Deuteronomy ends with Moses's death and Joshua taking the mantle of leadership. The book of Joshua recounts his guiding of Israel into the promised land of Canaan, which was divided between the twelve tribes of

Israel. These tribes were governed by a series of judges for several centuries. Samuel, the last judge, ushered in the period of the united monarchy under the reigns of Saul, David, and Solomon.

The kingdom split under Solomon's son Rehoboam, and the sovereign state of Israel became a nation divided. The house of Israel, known as the Northern Kingdom, consisted of ten tribes to the north, and the remaining two tribes made up the house of Judah, known as the Southern Kingdom. Because of Israel's flagrant idolatry, God appointed Assyria to defeat and scatter the people in 722 BC. Judah fared slightly better but also ultimately turned away from the Lord. The Babylonians devastated Jerusalem in 586 BC and hauled most of the remaining Jews off to Babylon.

In 538 BC, following the Persian conquest of Babylon, the Persian king, Cyrus, issued a decree allowing the dispersed Jews to move back to Jerusalem, rebuild the temple, and reestablish their sacrificial system. According to 2 Chronicles 36:22 and Ezra 1:1, this fulfilled the words of the prophet Jeremiah. In the years after Cyrus's decree, three waves of Jewish exiles returned to Jerusalem under the leadership of Zerubbabel (Ezra 1–6), Ezra (Ezra 7–10), and Nehemiah (Nehemiah 1–13).

But some Jews chose to stay in the land of their exile. The events recorded in the book of Esther took place in the city of Susa, some nine hundred miles from Jerusalem. Chronologically, they occurred between chapters 6 and 7 of Ezra. The book of Esther serves two purposes. First, to demonstrate God's faithfulness to his people no matter where they are. Second, to describe the origins of the Jewish feast of Purim.

ANCIENT SUSA AND THE WORLD OF ESTHER

All that remains of ancient Susa sits on the outskirts of a town called Shush in western Iran. In Esther's day, however, the city bore the reputation of one of the most important geographical sites in the ancient Near East. Our earliest Sumerian records tell of Susa passing through the hands of the Elamites, Assyrians, and Babylonians. King Cyrus conquered the city in approximately 540 BC, ushering its inhabitants into Persian rule.

Susa ascended to a place of prominence under the reign of Darius, commonly known as Darius the Great, from 522 BC until his death in 486 BC. He declared Susa the capital of his empire and began building a palace of extravagant splendor. The Persian king enlisted the efforts of the entire empire, importing cedar, gold, silver, ivory, and a vast array of precious stones. Perched atop an artificially constructed hill, the structure spanned nearly twelve and a half acres. Builders came from Egypt, Ethiopia, India, and modern-day Afghanistan. Darius spared no expense. When Xerxes, Darius's son, took the throne, he made this palatial estate his home. The book of Esther opens in the court of the palace garden. The author describes its opulence—curtains of fine linen, goblets of gold, floors made of precious gems. In fact, out of all the places recounted in Scripture, only the tabernacle and Jerusalem temple receive such detailed treatment.

King Xerxes was the most wealthy, powerful, and prominent man in the world. But he lacked wisdom. He surrounded himself with fools and made rash, impulsive, alcohol-induced decisions that caused problems not only for himself but also for the empire at large.

Esther entered the story as a young orphan torn from her uncle's home and thrust into the king's harem through no choice of her own. But God's invisible, providential hand guided her through what looked like chance events. Although the Lord is never mentioned in the book of Esther, he was ever near, faithfully keeping his promise to his covenant people, even when they lived outside of both the land and his will.

Divine Providence Set in Motion

LESSON 1

Recently, one of my (Sue's) friends was forced to leave her dream job as a women's minister of a large, prosperous church and move thousands of miles away to a tiny town in the middle of nowhere. Her husband's company made the move necessary, and she felt stuck and alone in a place where no one knew her, recognized her spiritual gifts and expertise, or seemed to care. I grieved with her and could relate.

In 1988, midway through my seminary degree, I heard my husband's car pull into the garage in the middle of the morning. "How strange," I thought. "What's he doing home at this hour?" Dazed, he explained that his company had laid off all employees with little explanation and sent everyone home.

For several months, he scoured the engineering job market in Dallas where we lived, but after a plethora of interviews, he experienced one door after another closing. Discouraged, he sent résumés to other cities and almost immediately, an exciting opportunity appeared—in *Austin*! No! God had called me to Dallas Theological Seminary. There were no seminaries I could attend in Austin! I loved teaching God's Word. My lifeblood was seeing women transformed into all-in, on-fire Jesus followers. Seminary equipped me to minister better. Surely this could not be God's will for me or our family.

I argued with my husband daily, giving every reason why this move would be a huge mistake. The kids initially balked, but eventually they were also excited, especially after we put a contingent contract down on a spacious, beautiful home tucked away in the Austin hills. I, however, remained resistant and resentful.

One morning I was driving to class and ranting about the unfairness of it all. Suddenly tears flooded my eyes and intense sobs forced me to pull off the highway. After a lengthy ugly cry, I prayed, "Okay, Lord, if this is your will, I'll accept it. I don't understand why you would provide this

OPTIONAL

Memorize Romans 11:33-36

Oh, the depth of the riches of the wisdom and knowledge of God! How unsearchable his judgments, and his paths beyond tracing out! "Who has known the mind of the Lord? Or who has been his counselor?" "Who has ever given to God, that God should repay them?" For from him and through him and for him are all things. To him be the glory forever! Amen.

opportunity to study your Word with some of the most renowned and godly scholars in the world and then yank it away. But help me to trust you and place the needs of my family first." That afternoon I arrived home with my attitude adjusted and ready to move forward into our new adventure.

Except the next day, my husband discovered that the boss in Austin had misled him, and my husband backed out of the position. The day after that, he received a call from the business that bought out his former company. They offered him his old job back with a sizable raise. We weren't moving after all, and I could stay in seminary! And fortunately, the contract on the Austin house was easily voided. I was ecstatic and grateful. I praised God for allowing me to continue my education, which ultimately led to joyful service on that seminary faculty for almost two and a half decades.

As I've looked back on this experience, I've sensed God was teaching me to trust him, helping me overcome my stubborn willfulness and my desire to have my own way. Yet as I walked beside my grieving friend, I observed her struggling to praise God in her current situation. For her, it felt like God hadn't worked everything out for good. But does her situation mean that God loves her less than he loves me? No. He is simply guiding her on a different path, one we aren't able to see or understand right now. Author Chuck Swindoll writes,

> God is in sovereign control . . . in the events of our own day. In the midst of those very circumstances that today have you baffled, wondering what you're going to do, or even how you're going to go on, you can rest assured that God's power and sovereign control are already at work. God never knows frustration. He never has to scratch His head, wondering what in the world He's going to do next with people like us, or with the nations of this world.[1]

The lifework God has planned for my friend is yet to unfold, but we can trust that it's going to be in her best interest. I can't wait to see what he has in store and cheer for her. Similarly, in this study of Esther, we will observe God's sovereign control over time at every turn in Esther's life and in the rescue of her people. Explore each episode of this upcoming saga and internalize the reality that God was in control of Esther's life, and he's in control of yours too.

THE STORY'S SETTING

Xerxes I, commonly known as Xerxes the Great (referred to in the Hebrew text as Ahasuerus), ruled Persia from 486 BC until his assassination in 465 BC. He wielded more power than any other man on earth, and his vast empire stretched from modern Pakistan in the east to modern Turkey in the west. Yet he wasn't content until he conquered his rivals to the west: the Greeks. We enter this true account with Xerxes hosting a series of banquets in conjunction with war councils to solidify support for his upcoming military campaign. These councils and parties were designed to persuade his subjects to finance, support, and serve as soldiers in his military plot to annihilate his Greek enemies. Among his subjects were many exiled Jews who had the opportunity to return home but had preferred to remain in the comfort of the lives they had built in Persia.

1. Theologian Karen Jobes writes that "God's will for an individual's life is unfolded through divine providence day by day."[2] Do you agree and, if so, how does that look in your life? If not, what are your related struggles and questions?

2. If you can think of an example of divine providence, a time when you knew God was at work in your life, share it with the group.

3. How can we become more attuned to perceiving God's divine providence in our lives? Consider the following verses for insight:

   Acts 17:26–27

   Romans 8:28–30

God used the Persian ruler Cyrus to free the Jews from captivity. In 538 BC Cyrus issued a decree that allowed the Jews to return to Jerusalem and to rebuild their temple using Persian resources. However, most of the Jews chose not to uproot. Some fifty years later, Esther and many other Jews remained in the comfort of the thriving cities in Persia. What was the status of the Jews who refused to return? Were they still a part of the covenant community? Did they obey the law and observe temple sacrifices and rituals? If not, were they still God's chosen people? We will dig into these questions and discover answers over the course of this study.

DIGGING DEEPER

Study Ezra 1:1–11. What do you learn about King Cyrus, the Jewish exiles, and the sovereignty of God?

DIGGING DEEPER

If you struggle with understanding God's divine providence and how it relates to our free will, consider reading this excellent resource: J. I. Packer, *Evangelism and the Sovereignty of God* (IVP, 2012).

Proverbs 16:33

Acts 16:6–7

Archaeologists excavating at Susa have unearthed inscriptions in which this king refers to himself as, "The great king. The king of kings. The king of the lands occupied by many races. The king of this great earth." Old Ahaseurus [Xerxes] didn't struggle with an inferiority complex![3]
—Charles Swindoll

DIVINE PROVIDENCE TO PROTECT THE JEWS BEGINS

 **Read Esther 1:1–8.**

4. During the first six months of the third year of Xerxes's reign, he hosted a series of extravagant banquets. Who was invited (vv. 2–4)? What gender were all his guests (v. 8)?

DIGGING DEEPER

In the second chapter of Daniel, Nebuchadnezzar (the king of Babylon before Darius and Xerxes were kings in Persia) had a dream that predicted four future kingdoms (Daniel 2:31–45). Decipher which of the four kingdoms in the dream is the Medo-Persian Kingdom, the vast empire ruled by Xerxes. What can you learn about God's divine providence over history?

5. Who else did Xerxes invite to the final feast that lasted seven days (v. 5)?

6. Imagine you were invited to this final feast. What would have impressed you the most about the king's garden party (vv. 6–7)?

7. What did Xerxes do that resulted in an atmosphere of revelry and ultimately drunken debauchery at his garden party (v. 8)?

Persia's wealth and magnificence dazzled even [the Greek ruler] Alexander the Great when more than a century later [after Xerxes's reign] he entered the palace at Susa and found 40,000 talents of gold and silver bullion (1,200 tons) and 9,000 talents of minted gold coins (270 tons).[4]
—Karen Jobes

Read Esther 1:9–12.

8. What was going on inside the royal palace during the party (v. 9)?

Biblical scholars differ concerning the king's request. Some conjecture he commanded Vashti to appear unveiled; others suggest that he requested she appear wearing only her crown. Whatever the request, the queen realized she would be paraded as a sexual object before a crowd of drunken men, and she refused.

9. On the last day of the festivities, what did the king request to top off the men's entertainment (vv. 10–11)? What do you think motivated such a rash decision? What was he hoping to accomplish?

Ancient Persian kings castrated some of the males who served in their courts. The eunuchs could not have children, so they were less likely to attempt to overthrow the king or engage in political plots for the benefit of their own family dynasties. The royal lineage would not be threatened by potential rivals. In addition, eunuchs who worked in the king's harem could be trusted not to become enamored with his concubines or wives.

10. Through the ages, some readers have condemned the queen, insisting that she should have submitted to her husband's request, while others have lauded her for her refusal. What do you think and why?

11. The Bible teaches believers to seek to become people characterized by the fruit of the Spirit: love, joy, peace, forbearance, kindness, goodness, faithfulness, gentleness, and self-control (Galatians 5:22–23).

When Persian kings dine, their legal wives sit beside them and share the feast. But if they [the men] want to amuse themselves or get drunk, they send their wives away, and summon the singing-girls and the concubines. And they are quite right not to share their drunken orgies with their wives. So, if a private citizen, intemperate and tasteless in his pleasures, commits an offense with a mistress or maidservant, his wife ought not to be angry or annoyed, but reflect that it is his respect for her that makes her husband share his intemperance or violent behavior with another woman.[5]

—Plutarch

DIGGING DEEPER

Study Ephesians 5:21–33 and write a response on how this text teaches married couples to relate to one another.

Another way to refer to these beautiful qualities is a submissive spirit that acts with the best interest of others in mind. If the married couple Xerxes and Vashti had exhibited submissive spirits toward one another, how might the outcome have been different?

12. How did Xerxes respond when he heard that Vashti refused his command to appear at his banquet as his trophy wife (v. 12)?

 Read Esther 1:13–22.

13. Xerxes wasn't sure what to do with Vashti after she embarrassed him publicly. Who did he consult? What do you learn about them in verses 13–15?

14. Memukan, the lead adviser, spoke for the group in verses 16–18. What did these men fear? In your opinion, why?

15. What were Memukan's two suggestions in verse 19?

16. How would the second suggestion later illustrate God's divine providence in saving the Jews?

Don't fall into the trap of thinking that God is asleep when it comes to nations, or that He is out of touch when it comes to carnal banquets, or that He sits in heaven wringing His hands when it comes to godless rulers (and foolish presidents!) who make unfair, rash, or stupid decisions. Mark it down in permanent ink: God is always at work. But His ways are so different from ours.[6]
—Charles Swindoll

17. What did the king and his advisers hope to accomplish through this irrevocable royal decree (v. 20)?

In Esther 1:13–22, respect is demanded from the Persian wives by order of royal decree; in Ephesians 5, respect is to be the response of a woman toward a man who loves her as Christ loved the church and gave himself up for her.[7]
—Karen Jobes

18. Can respect be won by force or power? How does someone gain respect? In your opinion, was the royal edict likely to accomplish what the king and his advisers hoped for?

How did this massive empire communicate without cell phones? The American West was not the first to use dispatch systems like the Pony Express. Messengers on horseback speedily relayed the king's royal edict from place to place until all citizens knew about this new law.

19. After Xerxes issued the edict, what was required for him to inform his vast empire (v. 22)?

20. If you were a Persian wife living in Xerxes's empire, how do you think you would have responded when the king's edict was read to you? Why?

21. What began as an issue between a married couple and their banquet guests had escalated into a national "talk of the town." In the king's attempt to save face, how did his edict actually backfire?

22. After dissecting this historical account, what words would you use to describe King Xerxes's character?

23. How would you rate the king's expertise and wisdom in ruling his empire and why?

24. Although Xerxes would be a great candidate for one of the worst world leaders, how did God use him to enact divine future purposes?

"My thoughts are not your thoughts, neither are your ways my ways," declares the LORD. "As the heavens are higher than the earth, so are my ways higher than your ways and my thoughts than your thoughts."
—Isaiah 55:8–9

25. When you observe current political rulers making foolish choices, can you trust that God is using what looks unfathomable to accomplish his perfect future purposes? If so, what helps you maintain this trust? If not, what hinders you? (Please refrain from discussing specifics about politics.)

THE THEME OF DIVINE PROVIDENCE IN ESTHER

The theme of divine providence pervades the book of Esther. Karen Jobes defines God's providence this way: "When we speak of God's providence, we mean that God, in some invisible and inscrutable way, governs all creatures, actions, and circumstances through the normal and the ordinary course of human life, without the intervention of the miraculous."[8] Elsewhere Jobes writes, "The major theological point of Esther is that throughout history God fulfills his covenant promises through his providence. . . . God's will for an individual's life is unfolded through divine providence day by day."[9]

Throughout this study, be on the lookout for ways God secretly shows us "that beneath the surface of even seemingly insignificant human decisions and events, an unseen and uncontrollable power is at work that can be neither explained nor thwarted."[10] As Jobes also puts it: "Like Xerxes of long ago, modern kings, presidents, and rulers make decisions from purely political motives. . . . These events may be completely secular and perhaps made by people who give Christ no thought. Nonetheless, through them God is moving all of history forward to accomplish all that must happen before the return of his Son, Jesus Christ, the true King of kings."[11]

Divine Providence Through Pagan Rulers

LESSON 2

Has God recently lost control of world events? Some might think so in light of the quality of the world leaders who dominate the twenty-first-century political scene and the resulting division and chaos. However, thousands of years ago, Solomon wrote, "The king's heart is in the hand of the Lord, like the rivers of water; He turns it wherever He wishes" (Proverbs 21:1 NKJV). True then and true now, even for the hearts of politicians.

For example, in 538 BC, the pagan King Cyrus freed the Jews after seventy years of captivity in Babylon and Persia.

> In the first year of Cyrus king of Persia, in order to fulfill the word of the LORD spoken by Jeremiah, the LORD moved the heart of Cyrus king of Persia to make a proclamation throughout his realm and also to put it in writing:
>
> "This is what Cyrus king of Persia says:
>
> "'The LORD, the God of heaven, has given me all the kingdoms of the earth and he has appointed me to build a temple for him at Jerusalem in Judah. Any of his people among you may go up, and may the LORD their God be with them.'" (2 Chronicles 36:22–23)

Mordecai, Esther, and the Jews still residing in Persia chose not to uproot even though they were free to return home as instructed. Nevertheless, God continued to care for them.

God's sovereign hand directs earthly events despite the anti-Semitism we'll see later in our study, despite the hostility toward Jews and Christians today, and despite the spiritual immaturity of world leaders. We can trust that King Jesus controls the unfolding of history and that all kingdoms will ultimately bow to his righteous reign. Let this reality soothe your soul and temper your response to politics.

OPTIONAL

Memorize Psalm 2:1–6

Why do the nations conspire and the peoples plot in vain? The kings of the earth rise up and the rulers band together against the LORD and against his anointed, saying, "Let us break their chains and throw off their shackles." The One enthroned in heaven laughs; the Lord scoffs at them. He rebukes them in his anger and terrifies them in his wrath, saying, "I have installed my king on Zion, my holy mountain."

In this book we have Israel in what was really a self-chosen path, for opportunity had been given to return to the land of their fathers, there to rebuild the city of God, but they preferred to remain where they were rather than endure the hardship of emigrating to Canaan. They were in Persia and Babylon when they might have been in Palestine, gathered around God's center at Jerusalem.[1]

—H. A. Ironside

Then the family heads of Judah and Benjamin, and the priests and Levites—everyone whose heart God had moved—prepared to go up and build the house of the LORD in Jerusalem. All their neighbors assisted them with articles of silver and gold, with goods and livestock, and with valuable gifts, in addition to all the freewill offerings.
—The prophet Ezra (1:5-6)

When asked, "Which political party more closely follows the teaching of Jesus and why?" one forum writer said,

> Jesus distanced himself from all of that, utterly refusing affiliation with ANY of the political power structures. . . .
>
> At the same time I don't believe that Jesus-followers should shun politics. To shed moral and compassionate light in our society, particularly the dark halls of our parliaments and legislative assemblies is a good thing, a way to be a positive influence, but to think that Jesus has any kind of political affiliation or would endorse a particular political party is misguided. His message transcends bills, constitutions, political debates and rallies. Instead he is all about transforming the lives of individual people through grace and forgiveness, through the power of his Spirit in our hearts and lives. Nothing is more world-changing than that.[2]

If you are allowing politics to control your peace of mind, look up, behold your God, and fill your mind with biblical truth. Remember, if God used the pagan King Cyrus to direct history to his desired end on behalf of the Jews, he can use any secular politician for his purposes on behalf of believers today.

DIGGING DEEPER

Read Isaiah 44:24–45:13 to understand more about God's relationship with the pagan ruler Cyrus. What do you learn about God's sovereignty over world affairs, even through nonbelievers?

BEAUTY AND THE BACHELOR (OR BEAST?)

Read Esther 2:1–4.

Despite all Xerxes's planning and conniving to raise formidable military forces to conquer the Greeks, they defeated his Persian army in the Battles of Thermopylae and Salamis (481–479 BC). Almost four years have passed and Xerxes has returned home with his tail between his legs.

1. Describe King Xerxes's mood in verse 1. Can you discern why he might have felt that way?

2. What did the king's personal attendants propose? What qualities were they looking for in a new queen? (vv. 1–4)

Do you agree or disagree with the assessment by Charles Swindoll here? "Ahasuerus enters the tall, gilded palace doors, weary from battle, dispirited by defeat. He longs for someone to greet him with arms outstretched, someone who will offer words of comfort and understanding. Not just a servant or one of his officers eager to please the king, but someone who truly cares for him and his feelings. Perhaps for the first time this monarch knows true defeat and loneliness."[3]

3. What does this proposal reveal about the status and value of women in the Persian Empire?

4. The king could have had any woman he wanted at any time. Why do you think this plan appealed to him?

He [Xerxes] dallied with the wives of some of his officers, sowing an anger that led to his assassination in his bedroom in 465 B.C.[4]
—Karen Jobes

5. Like Xerxes, have you ever made a decision in anger that you regretted when you cooled down? If so, share the experience with the group. What did you learn?

This method of selecting a queen is unorthodox, to say the least: typically, a queen would be chosen only from an aristocratic family, in order to create or reaffirm political alliances. Xerxes' own mother, Atossa, was daughter of none other than Cyrus the Great (*Hist.* 3.88). But under the circumstances, this method might have been considered appropriate. Vashti had lost her position because she had not shown proper submission to the king. Her replacement would not be apt to do likewise.[5]
—Anthony Tomasino

TWO JEWS SECRETLY AND PROVIDENTIALLY ENTER THE SCENE

Read Esther 2:5–7.

6. What do you learn about Mordecai from verses 5 and 6?

DIGGING DEEPER

Second Kings 24:8–16 provides details concerning the Babylonians' enslavement of the Jews that began the Jews' seventy-year captivity in foreign lands as a result of worshipping other gods. It's likely that Mordecai or his ancestors were taken at this time. How do you think this experience might have shaped Mordecai to step into a leadership role in the book of Esther?

7. What do you learn about Hadassah, also known by her Persian name Esther, from verse 7?

8. How likely was it for a Jewish orphan to become the next queen of Persia? How did God use the advisers' shortsighted contest parameters to benefit Esther?

Our main character has two names: her Jewish name, Hadassah, and her Gentile name, Esther. Daniel and his friends were also assigned pagan names by their captors in Babylon to indicate their assimilation into the culture. In Esther's case, her pagan name hid her identity as a Jew until that revelation was wise.

HUMAN TRAFFICKING ON STEROIDS

Read Esther 2:8–11.

9. In verse 8, what happened to Esther and many of the most beautiful young virgins in the empire? How do you think being involuntarily taken from their homes, families, and everything familiar might have affected them? How do you think you might have reacted?

10. We learn in verse 10 that Mordecai had forbidden Esther to reveal that she was Jewish. Why do you think he was so insistent?

11. What do the verses below teach about showing favoritism? How can they apply to favoritism based on race or ethnicity?

Genesis 12:2–3

Ephesians 2:11–18

James 2:1–4, 8–9

12. How was God working on Esther's behalf in verse 9?

13. How did Mordecai stay informed concerning Esther's circumstances (v. 11)?

Below are useful terms you might not know:

Harem: A part of the palace where the king's wives or concubines lived.

Concubine: A wife or sexual partner with second-class status, a mistress. In Esther, concubines lived in the harem, available for the sexual pleasure of the king.

Eunuch: A castrated man. In Esther, one of these officials was in charge of the king's harem. He could be trusted because he could not experience sexual temptation.

DIGGING DEEPER

In Genesis 15, God made a covenant concerning the promised land with Abram (later known as Abraham), the father of the Jewish people (see also Genesis 17:1–8). How did God ratify the covenant? Was it conditional or unconditional? How does this covenant relate to what's happening in the Middle East today?

Only wealthy Persian women could afford oils and perfumes produced in Persia or imported from India and Arabia. Archaeologist W. F. Albright discovered cube-shaped containers in Israel that he believes were used by women for beauty treatments. They would heat aromatic spices and oils in the containers until they steamed, then crouch over the burner to allow the fragrance to penetrate their skin. He cites Esther 2:12 as a biblical example and suggests this practice was common in the ancient Near East.[6]

DIGGING DEEPER

Read Daniel 1:3–16 and compare and contrast how foreign leaders treated Daniel and Esther. How did they respond differently to the special treatment they each received? How did the obedience of Esther and the disobedience of Daniel both move God's plan forward?

God's sovereignty was at work through the encounter of a pagan king and a Jewish virgin, for it would lead to the rescue of God's people.[7]
—Carl Anderson

GOD GUIDES THE KING'S HEART

Read Esther 2:12–18.

This scene could be compared to the most extreme version of the TV reality show *The Bachelor*. Even today some women are willing to go through extended beauty treatments to compete with one another for a man's love. However, much more is at stake in this true-to-life drama.

14. Do you often compare yourself to other attractive women? What emotions do you think these young women might have felt as they competed for the royal crown?

15. Each young virgin was allowed to take "anything she wanted" from the harem into the king's bedchamber (v. 13). What did Esther take, and what do you learn about her from this decision (vv. 15–16)?

16. We don't know whether Esther had been raised with Jewish moral standards—standards that would prevent her from marrying a non-Jew. Yet she was forced into intimate relations with an uncircumcised man she had never met. Why do you think she submitted to this ordeal? How do you think you would have reacted if you had been Esther?

17. What happened to Esther and the other young women after their night with the king (vv. 13–14)? What would be their designated title now, unless the king desired to see them again? What would this mean for all but one of these young women's futures?

Esther must have eaten, dressed and lived like a Persian, thus breaking Jewish dietary laws and other customs. Presumably this was because Mordecai felt her Jewish descent would lessen her chances of becoming queen. Some have criticized her as being "worldly-wise", but this seems a harsh judgment in the light of the circumstances that prevailed at the time.[8]
—John Bendor-Samuel

18. The king chose Esther as his queen! Think back over what you've learned from Esther 1 and 2 so far. Now list the many ways God moved to make this happen.

All the women gathered were now, essentially, either wives or concubines of the king. They might have sexual relations with him only once—on the night when they were brought into his presence—but they were not to have sexual relations with any other man . . . the king was taking all the most beautiful women from the entire empire, spending only a single night with most of them, and then sequestering them away from the company of men. . . . While many women might have found the life of luxury that these young ladies would receive to be enviable, the male audience would surely have found this arrangement distasteful. The king was taking all the best women for himself, leaving only those women who were not deemed "beautiful" for the rest of the men in the empire to fight over.[9]
—Anthony Tomasino

19. If you can recall a time when you felt like the favor of the Lord was with you, share it with the group.

WAS ESTHER PARTICIPATING IN A BEAUTY PAGEANT?

In eighth grade, my (Rebecca's) friend Nicole entered the junior Miss Minnesota pageant. As a thirteen-year-old, I had no experience with the world of beauty contests and watched, wide-eyed and a wee bit envious, as Nicole met with makeup artists, fashion consultants, and modeling coaches.

Finally, the day arrived. She answered every question articulately, performed her dance routine flawlessly, and glided down the runway like a princess in her white ball gown. At the end of the three-hour production, the audience waited breathlessly, hoping to hear their candidate's name. "And the new Junior Miss Minneapolis is . . ." Shrieks and screams erupted

Regardless of their character, their motives, or their fidelity to God's law, the decisions Esther and Mordecai make move events in some inscrutable way to fulfill the covenant promises God made to his people long ago.[10]
—Karen Jobes

Do not forget this one thing, dear friends: With the Lord a day is like a thousand years, and a thousand years are like a day.
—The apostle Peter (2 Peter 3:8)

from her cheering section as the emcee announced her name to the orchestra's crescendo—Nicole won!

Confetti dropped from the ceiling. Nicole's hands flew to her face. The other contestants feigned smiles as the previous year's winner placed a crown on Nicole's head. Someone thrust a bouquet of roses into her hands. Not only did my friend claim the title, but she also received all sorts of prizes, scholarships, and opportunities. Looking back, it feels a bit like a fairy tale.

Perhaps you've heard the first few chapters of Esther taught in a similar fashion. Dallas Theological Seminary Professor Sandra Glahn says nothing could be further from the truth: "So, let us be clear: There is no true love between Esther, the beautiful girl chosen to replace Vashti, and the powerful king who chooses her. This is a guy who rounds up virgins, tries them out, and picks his wife on the basis of her sexual performance and her looks. Oh, and she must be a virgin before he has his way with her."[11]

Esther's story takes place in a pagan setting where women could be taken or discarded at will. But God's sovereign hand is firmly in place, even if his fingerprints can't be seen.

Divine Providence Behind the Curtain

LESSON 3

OPTIONAL

Memorize Isaiah 50:10

Who among you fears the LORD and obeys the word of his servant? Let the one who walks in the dark, who has no light, trust in the name of the LORD and rely on their God.

I (Rebecca) was a theater kid from elementary school through college. Although I suffered from generalized anxiety, something about the stage washed away my worries and made me feel confident and brave. I'll never forget the year our director chose *Into the Woods* for the spring musical. My heart was set on the role of Cinderella. The director promised to post the cast list by the end of the last period on Friday. The minutes dragged on like hours. Finally, the bell rang. Springing from my desk, I raced to the other end of the school, dodging and weaving through the crowd of students. Before I was close enough to read the names, one of the girls bear-hugged me and squealed. "You got it! You're Cinderella, and I'm your wicked stepmother!" Shrieking and laughing, we jumped up and down, high-fiving the rest of the cast.

Our director was a creative technical genius. The set rivaled Broadway's finest. However, it took a stage crew of ten to twelve people to move props around between scenes. The curtain would drop, the lights would dim, and to the audience, all would be still. From the outside, it looked like nothing was happening. But behind the curtain, the stage manager barked instructions. Actors raced to change costumes as the crew lowered a new backdrop. The crew removed furniture, and the stage transformed from the inside of a cabin to a lonely spot in the woods. All of this happened behind the scenes, concealed from the people in the seats, until the moment the curtain rose.

In Esther 2:19–3:15, God remained hidden while all Hades broke loose for the Jews. From the outside, it looked as though all was lost, with no hope. But behind the heavenly curtain, we will see that God remained as actively invested in his covenant people as he was when he led them through the Red Sea. Though opposition arose through the wicked Haman, God was sovereignly working and moving just out of sight to accomplish his purposes.

Read Esther 2:19–23.

1. Reread Esther 2:15–18 and briefly summarize what has happened in Esther's life. How do you imagine she felt after this series of events?

2. Read the first half of verse 19 and fill in the blanks.

   When the ____________________ were ____________________ a ____________________ time . . .

   What does this tell us about King Xerxes's approach to marriage?

   What does this tell us about the king's character?

3. Have you ever felt you were not good enough for a person or a task? Describe the situation.

4. The sting of rejection runs deep and can take years to overcome if left untended. It can leave us wounded and living in a state of insecurity instead of experiencing the joy of belonging. Read Ephesians 1:3–6. How do Paul's words encourage anyone experiencing rejection?

Throughout the Near East, law cases and official matters were handled near the gate area. Therefore, that Mordecai was "sitting at the king's gate" suggests that he was an official of some sort.[1]
—Mervin Breneman

5. Where was Mordecai when this second assembling of the virgins took place? Briefly reread 2:3–4. Would Mordecai have known this second assembly was happening?

6. Recall Mordecai's relationship with Esther (v. 7). How might he have felt knowing that, even though Esther had taken her place as queen, King Xerxes wanted to expand his harem?

7. What did Mordecai overhear? How did he react? What does this say about his character? (vv. 20–23)

DIGGING DEEPER

Read Matthew 5:43–48; Luke 23:34; Acts 7:60; and Romans 12:14–19. How might the examples of Jesus and Stephen inform how we respond when someone hurts us? How do Paul's words to the Roman Christians encourage us? If you are carrying bitterness or unforgiveness, write a prayer for the one who harmed you, asking the Lord to help you trust him for justice and offer forgiveness. (Note: If you have been severely violated or abused, please seek outside help. Illegal and abusive behavior should always be reported to the proper authorities. Forgiveness does not always necessitate reconciliation.)

Kings in the ancient world were always weary of assassination attempts, oftentimes from their own family members. Karen Jobes notes, "Acts of loyalty were usually rewarded immediately and generously by Persian kings," primarily to prevent attacks and encourage allegiance.[2]

[The ancient historian] Herodotus tells of King Xerxes, who had his secretaries record each time he saw one of his officers behaving with distinction during a battle against the Greeks.[3]
—Mervin Breneman

DIGGING DEEPER

Read Matthew 6:1–4. How do Jesus's words encourage those who feel their work goes unnoticed?

8. What did Queen Esther do in response to the information Mordecai relayed?

9. Although Mordecai and Esther may have felt slighted (or disgusted) over the king's lust, they both acted to save Xerxes from an assassination attempt. Have you ever found yourself in a situation where you sensed the Lord asking you to honor someone who had wounded you? What happened? How did you respond? Did the Lord minister to you in the situation? If so, how?

10. Verse 23 records two outcomes after Esther reported the eunuchs to the king. What were they? What did the king do for Mordecai in response to his loyalty?

Read Esther 3:1–11.

11. Notice the first three words in 3:1. What events is the narrator speaking of? Who would the book's original audience expect to be rewarded at this point in the story? Who received a reward instead? Put yourself in Mordecai's shoes. How would you feel at this slight?

12. Have you (or someone you love) ever been bypassed for a promotion for someone who hadn't worked as hard as you, or gone unrecognized in other ways? Perhaps your child lost a spot on a team to someone less skilled than them. Maybe someone else accepted credit for your idea. Share your story (without mentioning names) with the group. How did you respond? How did the situation resolve itself?

13. How is Haman identified? How did King Xerxes honor him? How did Mordecai respond? (vv. 1–2)

14. Verse 3 says the king's servants questioned Mordecai daily about why he wouldn't bow down to Haman. Finally, he answered them. Why wouldn't Mordecai obey the command to kneel before Haman (v. 4)?

15. What did Mordecai instruct Esther to do concerning her ethnicity? Why do you think Mordecai chose this moment to reveal his heritage?

DIGGING DEEPER

Read Exodus 17:8–16. What did the Lord tell Moses he would do to the Amalekites? Read 1 Samuel 15:1–35. How did Saul sin? What was God's response to his sin (v. 11)? How did God punish Saul (v. 28)?

King Xerxes honored Haman . . . elevating him and giving him a seat of honor *higher than that of all the other nobles* (v. 1). Honor is a limited commodity, and Haman's promotion forces a new pecking order in the court. The king commanded the other officials to acknowledge Haman's new superiority by kneeling down before him. Herodotus reports (*Hist.* 1.134) that such bowing was done extensively in the Persian court, since it marked social ranking.[4]

—Timothy Laniak

Fans of Shakespeare's *Romeo and Juliet* recall the blood feud between the Montagues (Romeo's family) and Capulets (Juliet's family). The animosity between the fictional households pales in comparison, however, to the enmity between Haman's and Mordecai's ancestors. Haman's identifier, "the Agagite," means he was a descendant of King Agag, an Amalekite ruler. The Amalekites were an ancient enemy of the Jews from all the way back to the Israelites' exodus.

DIGGING DEEPER

Skim Exodus 17:8–16; Deuteronomy 25:17–19; and 1 Samuel 15:1–9 for additional insight into why Mordecai refused to pay homage to Haman.

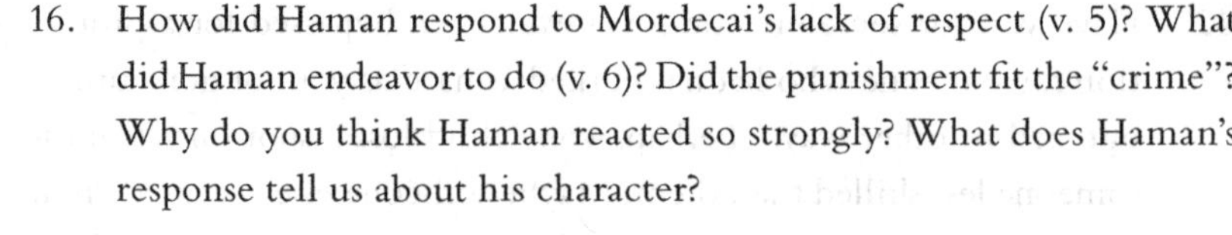

16. How did Haman respond to Mordecai's lack of respect (v. 5)? What did Haman endeavor to do (v. 6)? Did the punishment fit the "crime"? Why do you think Haman reacted so strongly? What does Haman's response tell us about his character?

Haman's name sounds something like the Hebrew word for wrath (Heb., *hemah*), an apt description of his temperament and role in this story. Once he knew that Mordecai was a Jew, Haman's pride-driven wrath was turned against all the Jewish people in the empire.[5]
—Karen Jobes

17. The text tells us that Haman next sought divine guidance through casting lots (Hebrew: *purim*). Who ultimately determined the outcome of the lots? Do you think this was a valid way of seeking God's will? Why or why not?

Because the Persians practiced Zoroastrianism during Xerxes's reign,[6] when casting lots, Xerxes was almost certainly seeking the favor of the pagan god Ahuramazda.

18. Today, millions of Americans seek spiritual guidance through tarot cards, palm reading, mediums, or fortune tellers. What does the Bible say regarding this practice (Deuteronomy 18:9–12)?

DIGGING DEEPER

In what month did Haman cast the lots (Esther 3:7)? What month did the lot fall on? Why was this month significant to the Jews (skim Exodus 12:1–12)? Put yourself in the original audience's shoes. Remember, they knew the story's outcome as they heard it read aloud. How might the date Haman chose to cast lots have amused them? Encouraged them?

19. On this side of Jesus's resurrection, we have someone far more trustworthy than tea leaf readers, spiritists, or those who cast lots. What is part of the Holy Spirit's role in our lives (John 16:13)? Why should this comfort us?

20. After King Xerxes's unsuccessful coup against the Greeks, his treasuries would have been low. Reread verses 8–11. How did Haman convince Xerxes to order an edict against the Jews (vv. 8–9)?

A talent of silver would weigh approximately seventy-five pounds, worth over twenty thousand dollars! Ten thousand talents meant Haman was offering King Xerxes over 205 million dollars to abolish the Jews!

21. How much investigating or fact-checking did King Xerxes do concerning this people group? What did he give Haman (v. 10)? What does this reiterate about Xerxes's character (see Esther 1:10–22)?

"Keep the money" (NIV) is literally "the silver is given to you," by which the king accepted the money but made it available for Haman to use.[7]
—Peter Lau

22. What descriptive term does the author add to Haman's name (v. 10)?

23. When Xerxes gave Haman his signet ring, he endowed him with almost unlimited authority, which Haman used to plot the genocide of the Jews. In what areas of life do you have authority? List them all in the space provided. How can you ensure that you use your influence and authority in a God-honoring way?

Read Esther 3:12–15.

24. The moment he slipped the king's signet ring onto his finger, Haman set his wicked plan in motion. To whom was the edict written (v. 12)? List every person and group mentioned in the text.

25. Where were the letters sent and whom did they affect? What did the letters instruct the hearers to do? (v. 13)

26. Paul told the Christians in Ephesus that "our struggle is not against flesh and blood, but against the rulers, against the authorities, against the powers of this dark world and against the spiritual forces of evil in the heavenly realms" (Ephesians 6:12). What does this tell us about Haman? How should this knowledge shape how we pray for those who come against us?

27. Haman wrote his decree on the thirteenth day of the first month—the night before the Jewish Passover. By lot, Haman determined that the day of destruction would be the thirteenth day of the twelfth month—eleven months in the future. How would that affect the

Jews' relationships with their neighbors? What might the Jews be able to do throughout that time?

28. How did the people of Susa respond to the decree? What did the king and Haman do after the decree was sent? (v. 15) How do you think you would respond?

29. How have you observed the "unseen hand" of God moving behind the scenes thus far in the story?

IN THEIR SHOES

Imagine the scene. You are lugging your wares home from the marketplace when you hear the town crier off in the distance. "Attention," he hollers. "All citizens must report to the square immediately for an urgent message from the king." Exhausted from a long day and dismayed at your sales, you sigh. A germ of anxiety takes root in your stomach and begins to grow. With a furrowed brow, you change course and follow the crowd. The closer you get, the more you notice—hushed whispers. Furtive looks. Suspicion. Fear. And then, shouting. Shoving. Panic.

Forgetting your cart, you worm your way up to the wall. Then you see it. Except that your eyes can't make sense of it. Your mind refuses to process the words. You read them two, then three, then four times. Someone shoves you from the side, breaking your near-trancelike state.

Destroy. Kill. Annihilate. All Jews. In one day. Young and old. Women and children.

Your children! You race back to your cart, call your children's names, and breathlessly fight your way home. The kids, sensing your anxiety, ask you what's wrong. Once friendly and welcoming, your neighbors' faces now pose only threats.

We can easily understand how the Jews living in Persia during Xerxes's reign would have felt. One author, writing of the mistreatment of German Jews in the time of the Holocaust, says,

> Teenagers also played a role in many communities when they enjoyed their newfound power to harass with impunity Jewish classmates and their parents—adults to whom youth were generally taught to defer—thereby contributing to the targeted group's isolation. Many ordinary Germans became invested in the ongoing persecution after acquiring Jewish businesses, homes, or belongings sold at bargain prices or benefiting from reduced business competition as Jews were driven from the economy.[8]

Life essentially stopped for the Jews of the Holocaust as they spent each day terrified that the Gestapo would appear at their doors. In much the same way, the Persian Jews lived under a doomsday clock counting down ever closer to zero. Around the world today, Christians face similar fears. Some furtively hide their faith and wonder who they can trust.

But what about those of us living in the West? Esther's story beckons us to view issues of justice through the eyes of Christ. Who are the oppressed in our towns and cities? Who are the voiceless? The powerless? The broken? The rejected? How will we respond when faced with the opportunity to do the right thing at great cost to ourselves?

Christians today can draw strength as they abide in Jesus and remember his words: "Do not be afraid of those who kill the body but cannot kill the soul. Instead, fear the one who is able to destroy both soul and body in hell" (Matthew 10:28 NET). Jesus also told his disciples, "Whenever you are arrested and brought to trial, do not worry beforehand about what to say. Just say whatever is given you at the time, for it is not you speaking, but the Holy Spirit" (Mark 13:11). Indeed, the one who stands for justice always stands with Christ.

Divine Providence in the Turbulence

LESSON 4

I (Rebecca) will never forget the day we buried my friend's brother. I had raced across town from work to attend the memorial service, arriving a few minutes late. Trying my best to slip in unnoticed, I sat in the back row of the packed church. Flowers filled every free space. A large framed portrait of the deceased beamed at us in front of a gleaming mahogany casket. The Scripture reader quietly took her place in the second row, and a hush descended over the room as the pastor took the stage.

"We are not mourning!"

My eyes widened as his voice thundered, echoing around the room.

"This is not an occasion for grieving. Today, we are celebrating the life of our brother in Christ as he crosses the threshold of eternity!"

Someone hollered, "Amen!"

I, however, couldn't believe my ears. My friend's brother had died under tragic circumstances at just forty-three years old. He left behind a doting wife and two children under the age of five. My friend and her family were devastated. How could the pastor tell us not to grieve?

The scenario I've described plays out across the country every day. For some reason, folks in the West have moved away from public opportunities to mourn and gravitated to a more celebratory ethos when loved ones pass on.

On the one hand, it makes sense. Paul reminded the church in Thessalonica that while we weep over our lost loved ones, we do not grieve like the rest of humanity, "who have no hope" (1 Thessalonians 4:13). On the other hand, the biblical authors embraced seasons of bereavement. Israel mourned for forty days when Moses died. Many of the poems in the book of Psalms were written as lament songs meant to be sung as a congregation. Jeremiah was known as the Weeping Prophet, and Jesus himself broke down at the gravesite of Lazarus. Stigmatizing grief and relegating it to the

OPTIONAL

Memorize Esther 4:14

If you remain silent at this time, relief and deliverance for the Jews will arise from another place, but you and your father's family will perish. And who knows but that you have come to your royal position for such a time as this?

Mordecai reacts with great emotion when he hears that the personal conflict between himself and Haman has brought the entire Jewish nation into jeopardy. Haman's plan to annihilate all the Jewish people is way out of proportion to Mordecai's offense. Apparently Mordecai's behavior had merely given Haman the excuse to put his power behind his anti-Semitism.[1]

—Karen Jobes

privacy of one's home robs us of the comfort found when we process our sorrow together.

I caught a glimpse of communal mourning when my Iranian neighbors lost their son. In stark contrast to forcing celebration, their friends surrounded them for nearly a month straight. When I went over to pay my respects, a group of women were sitting on the couch in silence, holding my neighbor's hand. Another woman read their sacred text aloud. The men scurried about managing household chores. Tears flowed freely. No one pasted silver-lining platitudes on my neighbors' broken hearts.

Esther 4 opens with a cacophony of lament. The Jews, having recently received word that the king had decreed their extermination, gathered together in groups to fast, wail, and weep.

A TIDAL WAVE OF TEARS

Read Esther 4:1–3.

Chapter 3 ended with the aftermath of Haman's edict to "destroy, kill and annihilate all the Jews" (v. 13). The author tells us that "the city of Susa was bewildered" (v. 15). Chapter 4 opens with a description of Mordecai's grief.

David writes, "The LORD is close to the brokenhearted and saves those who are crushed in spirit" (Psalm 34:18). When words fail to comfort, the presence of the Lord can bring peace. We have no power to save anyone, but we can certainly draw near to those who grieve and offer the ministry of a quiet, loving presence.

1. What did Mordecai do (vv. 1–2)?

2. Describe a time when you received painful news. How did you react? How did others react to you? If you are comfortable, share your experience with the group.

3. In verse 2, the author tells us that Mordecai stopped at the king's gate. Why? Why might the king have established this rule?

4. How did the Jews respond to Haman's edict? What does this tell us about the solidarity of their community? How do you think their response would have impacted their Persian neighbors?

5. What is your initial response when you see someone mourning?

SACKCLOTH AND ASHES

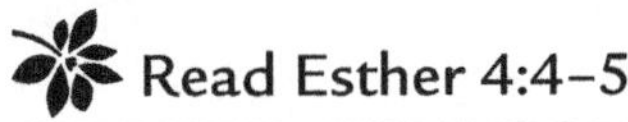

Read Esther 4:4–5.

6. What did Esther's servants tell her? How did Esther respond (v. 4)? Why do you think she responded that way?

Sackcloth was sometimes worn under the garments (2 Kings 6:30) in times of grief or as a belt or girdle (Isaiah 32:11), but Mordecai apparently wore an entire garment of the coarse cloth. He also covered himself in ashes, another typical way that people might make an external demonstration of their internal pain. Mordecai was making a public demonstration of his distress.[2]

—Anthony Tomasino

DIGGING DEEPER

Scholars suggest we hear sacred echoes of Joel's prophecies in Esther 4:3. The phrase "with fasting, weeping and wailing" occurs in both 4:3 and in Joel 2:12 (while English translators often use synonyms, the Hebrew construction of the phrase in Joel and Esther is identical), and similar phrases are frequently found throughout the Old Testament. Read Joel 2:12–14. How do these verses inform Mordecai's words to Esther in 4:13–14? How might they have influenced her response to Mordecai in verse 16?

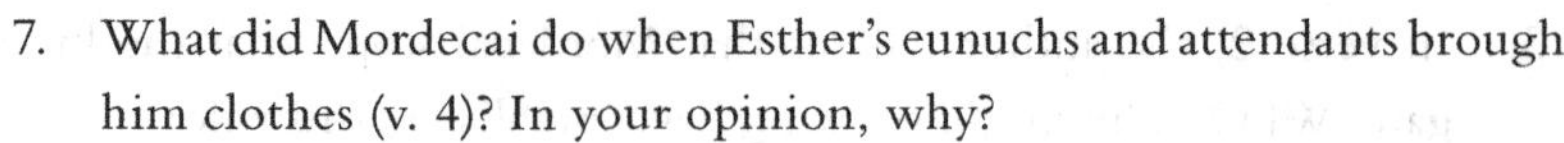

7. What did Mordecai do when Esther's eunuchs and attendants brought him clothes (v. 4)? In your opinion, why?

In the book of Esther, changes of clothing typically reflect a change in circumstances. For example, the Jews are clothed in sackcloth to signify their mourning (4:3); Esther puts on her royal robes before going to Xerxes, reminding him of her status as queen (5:1); Haman seeks to be clothed in royal robes as a sign of his own desire for honor (6:8–9); Mordecai is clothed in royal robes because the king wishes to honor him (6:10–11); Mordecai is clothed in royal robes to signify his promotion to vizier (8:10).[3]
—Anthony Tomasino

8. Upon his return, what did Esther want Hathak to find out (v. 5)?

9. What are some unhelpful ways Christians (unintentionally) attempt to "fix" someone's grief? What could we do instead?

A well-meaning college friend of mine (Rebecca) was quick with a joke or outrageous story anytime I went to her with a problem. Her noble intentions—to "fix" my problem by making me forget my pain—always left me feeling lonely and unseen. Instead of seeking to understand my broken heart, she wanted to make it go away. Unfortunately, grief left unprocessed has a way of rearing its head in unhealthy ways down the road.

10. Read Psalm 6:6–10. What did David do with his grief (vv. 6–8)? How did this change his attitude (vv. 9–10)?

DIGGING DEEPER

Read John 11:1–37. Summarize the story and especially Jesus's reaction to the news of Lazarus's death. What does this tell you about the heart of God and his response to the pain of this world? How might this story minister to someone in their grief?

ESTHER'S ONLY HOPE

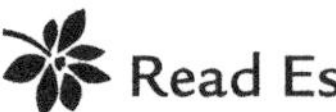

Read Esther 4:6–11.

11. What did Mordecai share with Hathak (v. 7)?

12. What does this exchange tell us about Esther's life and how often she interacted with people outside the palace?

Esther, in the seclusion of the harem, knew nothing of what the king and Haman had determined on. No one in the palace suspected how vitally she was concerned in the matter, since none knew that she was a Jewess, and state affairs are not commonly discussed between an Oriental monarch and a young wife.[4]
—George Rawlinson and J. R. Thomson

13. How connected are you with a local Christian community? Do you view deep communal ties as important? Why or why not?

This is a call to wake up to the fact that we can never realize the likeness of Christ by ourselves alone; we will never transform the world as individuals; we will never discover fullness of life in Christ if we stay solo. We are distinct as people of God because we were made to live in dependence on the head and interdependently with the diverse parts of the body.[5]
—Julie Gorman

14. What instructions did Mordecai give Hathak (v. 8)?

15. How did Esther respond to Mordecai (v. 11)? Why did she respond that way?

His dominion is an eternal dominion; his kingdom endures from generation to generation. All the peoples of the earth are regarded as nothing. He does as he pleases with the powers of heaven and the peoples of the earth. No one can hold back his hand or say to him: "What have you done?"
—King Nebuchadnezzar (Daniel 4:34-35)

16. King Xerxes had not called Esther to go to him for a month. What implication can we draw about the way he had been spending his nights?

17. Clearly, Esther feared for her life. What other emotions might she have been wrestling with?

18. Reread verse 11. What was Esther's only hope of gaining an audience with the king?

There is no attribute more comforting to His children than that of God's Sovereignty. Under the most adverse circumstances, in the most severe trials, they believe that Sovereignty has ordained their afflictions, that Sovereignty overrules them, and that Sovereignty will sanctify them all.[6]
—Arthur Pink

19. Read John 6:37 and Hebrews 10:19–23. In contrast to Esther, what kind of access do we have to the King of Kings and Lord of Lords? How should we live in light of this beautiful truth?

DIGGING DEEPER

Who do you most trust? Your closest friend? Your mother? Your husband? Chances are the person you trust the most is the one you know the best. Read the following passages: Isaiah 46:10; 49:14–16; and Jeremiah 29:10–13. If Esther had been intimately acquainted with God and his Word, how might her reaction in Esther 4:11–17 have reflected more trust?

IF I PERISH, I PERISH

Read Esther 4:12–17.

20. Glance back at 2:10. What had Mordecai commanded Esther *not* to do when she was taken into the king's harem?

21. Now that the fate of the Jews was on the line, Mordecai reversed his stance. Initially, Esther was reluctant to stand up for her people. Have you ever found yourself in a situation where you, as a Christian, were in the minority? If so, describe it. Were you ultimately open about your faith? Why or why not?

People who have hated God through the centuries have somehow found it in their hearts to hate the Jewish people. This sad fact is still true in our world today.[7]
—John Bisagno

22. Noticeably absent throughout the book is any mention of God or prayer. Now, however, we hear the faint strains of faith. What did Mordecai have the eunuchs tell Esther about her fate if she kept silent (vv. 13–14)?

What did Mordecai believe about the Jews' deliverance?

Why did Mordecai believe that Esther was chosen as queen?

23. The author of Hebrews writes that Jesus is "the pioneer and perfecter of faith" (12:2). God is also the pioneer and perfecter of our stories. Think back over the events of your life. Can you see how God has orchestrated them to bring you where you are now? If so, how?

DIGGING DEEPER

Read Acts 17:26–27 and think about where you live, shop, work, and get your hair done. What divinely ordained reason might God have for placing you where you are?

24. What trials or difficulties have you faced? How have they shaped your character? How have those situations impacted your relationship with God?

As you read, try to identify the ordinary, seemingly insignificant events God providentially used in significant ways to bring about an extraordinary outcome. Ask God to help you see how he is working in the everyday events in your life as well.[8]
—*Exploring Christian Scripture*

25. Up until this point in the story, Esther had been playing the role of a pawn—going where she was told to go and doing what she was told to do. Now, she was taking matters into her own hands. What did she tell Mordecai to do (v. 16)? In your opinion, why?

Fasting was usually for one day only. It was obligatory on the Day of Atonement (Lv. 16:29–31), but otherwise fasting was undertaken as a voluntary act for a particular occasion (1 Sa. 14:24; 2 Sa. 1:12). Esther's three-day fast indicated the seriousness with which she regarded the emergency and her own need of strength.[9]
—Joyce Baldwin

26. Although the text does not tell us that Mordecai trusted in God, most scholars and theologians believe that he showed faith when he claimed, "Relief and deliverance for the Jews will arise from another place" (v. 14). Often when one person shows great faith in dire circumstances, they inspire others to step out in faith as well. Can you think of someone who has shown deep faith in difficult times? What about them inspires you?

27. Mordecai wanted Esther to use her proximity to the king for the good of her people. Where in your life do you have power, prominence, or influence? How might you use it to impact people for Christ?

NOT AFRAID TO PERISH: THE STORY OF AHN EI SOOK

They call her a modern-day Esther. Ahn Ei Sook was two years old when Japan took control of Korea in 1910. Just as the Babylonians had displaced and deculturalized the Jews over two millennia earlier, Japanese officials sought to assimilate Koreans into their worldview and way of life. One source states:

> The Koreans were deprived of freedom of assembly, association, the press, and speech. Many private schools were closed because they did not meet certain arbitrary standards. The colonial authorities used their own school system as a tool for assimilating Korea to Japan, placing primary emphasis on teaching the Japanese language and excluding from the educational curriculum such subjects as Korean language and Korean history.[11]

Almost overnight, Koreans were forced to shift their religious allegiances to a syncretistic form of worship focused on deceased rulers, soldiers, and Japanese gods. Ei Sook, raised by a Christian mother and a pagan father, chose to follow Christ. She kept her Christian identity mostly hidden until one day, as a young teacher, she was forced to make a choice.

She stood with her students at the foot of the shrine to Amaterasu—the Japanese sun goddess. Whoever refused to bow would be forced into a prison cell where they would suffer torture and possibly death. Remembering Shadrach, Meshach, and Abednego from the book of Daniel, she silently prayed for strength. When a Japanese official called for attention and demanded that all pay homage to the mighty Amaterasu, every last person bowed. Except Ei Sook. She stood alone for Christ in the vast sea of people.

Shortly afterward, this brave young woman went into hiding. Knowing that prison awaited her, she began to train her body, sleeping on a cold floor, eating rotten food, and fasting days at a time. She also memorized Scripture—at first verses, then chapters, then whole books.

Then the authorities finally caught up with her. She was thrown into a cold, clammy cell next to a woman who screamed hysterically day and night. Ei Sook discovered the woman had viciously murdered her husband and was deemed insane. Ei Sook began to pray that the woman would be placed in her cell so that she could minister to her. God granted that prayer and many others during Ei Sook's six-year imprisonment. Through her steadfast love and faithfulness, not only did the mentally ill woman come to know Christ, but so did countless others, including many of Ei Sook's jailers.

In the Wisdom Literature, the phrase "who knows?" often has a sense of uncertainty or of something not able to be known (e.g., Prov 24:22; Eccl 2:19; 3:21). However, elsewhere in the OT the phrase is used in the context of hope in God's providence in a time of crisis, usually God's judgment (2 Sam 12:22; Joel 2:14; Jonah 3:9). This latter nuance better fits the context of Mordecai's sentence, "And who knows but that you have come to your royal position for such a time as this?"[10]

—Peter Lau

When Japan surrendered at the end of World War II, Ahn Ei Sook was finally released. She met and married a pastor named Dong Myun Kim. Ultimately, she and her husband moved to the United States, where they planted a church. Ei Sook changed her name to Esther, and to her dying day, she proclaimed that "to live for Christ means to die for Christ."[12]

Divine Providence in the Waiting

LESSON 5

LEARNING TO WAIT

By Jenica McMaster

OPTIONAL

Memorize James 5:7–8

Be patient, then, brothers and sisters, until the Lord's coming. See how the farmer waits for the land to yield its valuable crop, patiently waiting for the autumn and spring rains. You too, be patient and stand firm, because the Lord's coming is near.

I have a "ready, fire, aim" approach to life instead of "ready, aim, fire." I'm task oriented and often impatient when I need to check something off my list. Recently I was reminded of my desperate need for patience.

Our family moved from a large city in Arizona to a small town in Montana, where the pace is distinctively slower. Before moving, I worked at a large church. There, our staff enjoyed wrestling together with hard theological doctrines and defending our beliefs. Several times, I confronted younger believers who were off in their understandings of Scripture. You could say that I'm passionate about the church holding the line on essential orthodoxy.

Fast-forward to our move. We checked out a church with vague mission and vision statements. We needed more clarity before we committed to this church, so we attended the meet and greet with the senior pastor to get some of our questions answered.

I admit that I went into that meeting wounded. I did not want to move to this town. I did not want to quit a job I loved. I did not want to join this church or any church in my new town. I wanted to go home. Initially I sat quiet in the meeting and listened to others' "fluffy" questions. Finally, I couldn't take it any longer. I spit out one question after another, many of which the pastor had no answer for, which further fanned my fire.

By the end, I didn't have a lot of answers, but I did severely damage any opportunity I might ever have to speak into that church community. If I had been patient and humble, waiting on the Lord to ask my questions, my voice would not have been so polarizing. I might actually have made friends.

Today, through social media, we can say anything on our minds to the whole world. How many times have you said or written something in anger or frustration that you later regretted? How many times have you been like me, charging into a new situation ready for battle before establishing the relational connection to speak with understanding and grace? Wisdom waits.

I'm learning to wait for permission from the Holy Spirit to speak, especially if my words are confrontational. I often pray Psalm 141:3 over myself: "Set a guard over my mouth, Lord; keep watch over the door of my lips." I want to be more aware of how God is working while I wait to act. I'm changing my approach from "ready, fire, aim" to "ready, pray, aim, pray, fire, pray." This requires dependence. When we are self-reliant, we easily rush the process. We lack patience and we often fail. Dependence requires humility to follow God and wait for his direction before we move.

Esther provides an excellent example of someone God used mightily because she exhibited abundant patience in response to an urgent threat. If you, like me, need to learn to be more patient, take your time and wring out this lesson. You won't regret it.

Read Esther 5:1.

Mordecai informed Esther that their people were going to be destroyed at the hands of her husband, the same husband who had not wanted to see her for at least a month (4:11). No doubt she felt hurt, fearful, and insecure—typical responses for many women in the midst of rejection. Despite those emotions, Esther called for others to fast with her, and in three days, after the heat of the moment passed, she put on her royal robes and approached the king.

1. Esther was not just approaching Xerxes uninvited; she would have been very aware of what had happened to Queen Vashti when the former queen went against his orders. How do you think you would react if asked to approach the king, even if it meant possible death?

The book of Esther is full of ironies. For example, Vashti risked her life by *not* appearing before the king while Esther risked her life by appearing before the king without invitation.

2. How might the fact that the king had not asked to see you in almost a month have impacted your decision?

3. We have all experienced rejection, and some of us have built walls of self-protection as a result. The fear of rejection can paralyze us and hinder our obedience. Read Ephesians 1:3–6 and Philippians 3:20–21. How could these verses give you courage amid rejection?

Two bas-reliefs [carvings where figures look three-dimensional] have been excavated from Persepolis showing a Persian king seated on his throne with a long scepter in his right hand. An attendant standing behind the throne is a Median soldier holding a large ax. The threat of death and the hope of life are equally present as Esther summons the courage to approach the king.[1]
—Karen Jobes

4. Esther responded to a serious threat to herself and her people. What do you tend to do in perilous situations? If you are a mom, how do you react if someone endangers your child?

5. What do the verses below teach you about how to practice patience in the midst of a threat?

Proverbs 15:18

Proverbs 25:15

Galatians 5:16–18, 22–25

She [Esther] simply put herself in a position where the king could see her standing in the court as he was sitting on his throne. An important principle is illustrated by this act. People who hope to be used by God must boldly put themselves in a position where God can work through them, rather than sitting back, doing nothing, passively hoping or waiting for God to do something.[2]
—Gary Smith

James 1:19

Read Esther 5:2–8.

6. What happened in verse 2 when the king saw Esther standing outside the throne room?

When Xerxes said he would give Esther anything she requested "up to half the kingdom," he didn't mean it literally. Royalty used this expression to communicate that they were in a generous mood. We see the same comment in Mark 6:23, centuries later, when Herod offered "up to half [his] kingdom" to Salome, who then requested the head of John the Baptist.

7. In verse 3, the king expressed great interest in why Esther was there, offering "up to half" his kingdom. Why do you think she didn't immediately tell him that she and all Jews were under a death sentence?

8. Esther could have invited the king to dinner alone. Asking Haman to join them meant including the very person who was threatening to kill her and her people. Why do you think Esther chose to also summon Haman?

These negotiations reveal that there is a right time and place to accomplish a task. . . . Unusual accomplishments are possible for those who have the wisdom and patience to wait for just the right time and place.[3]
—Gary Smith

9. During Esther's dinner party, the king again asked her what she wanted (v. 6). How did she respond (v. 8)? Any ideas why she waited a second time? What held Esther back twice?

Truth uttered before its time is always dangerous.
—Attributed to Mencius

Now this is her moment to bring down the roof on Haman—but she doesn't. Not now. This is a wise woman who understands the value of timing. She isn't in a hurry, nor is she revengeful. You know why? She has been *waiting* on the Lord.[4]
—Charles Swindoll

10. Have you ever found yourself in a situation similar to Esther's, where you needed to determine when to speak but, possibly for no apparent reason, felt hesitant? If so, what happened? Did you later understand the reason for waiting?

During a waiting period, God is not only working in our hearts, He's working in others' hearts. And all the while He is giving added strength.[5]
—Charles Swindoll

Read Esther 5:9–14.

11. What was Haman's mood as he left Esther's feast? Why? What happened to enrage him (v. 9)?

What is hastily asked is often as hastily denied; but what is asked with a pause deserves to be considered.[6]
—Matthew Henry

12. Have you ever allowed one person's sour attitude toward you to color your whole outlook and mood? If so, can you discern why? How might you overcome this tendency?

He gives strength to the weary and increases the power of the weak. Even youths grow tired and weary, and young men stumble and fall; but those who hope in the LORD will renew their strength. They will soar on wings like eagles; they will run and not grow weary, they will walk and not be faint.
—The prophet Isaiah (40:29–31)

DIGGING DEEPER

Read James 5:7–11 and Job 1–3 and 38–42. What can you learn about patience during adversity and suffering?

13. Why do you think Mordecai refused to honor Haman? What do you learn about Mordecai from this snub?

14. What do you learn about Haman from his initial reaction to Mordecai (vv. 9–10)?

15. When Haman arrived home, he gathered his friends and his wife and vomited his rage all over them. What did he talk about (vv. 11–12)? In your opinion, why? What else do you learn about Haman?

16. Do you ever resort to name-dropping or boasting about your accomplishments, even subtly? If so, when do you tend to do this? Can you discern why? What does this reveal about you? How can you subdue this propensity?

17. King Solomon wrote many proverbs to help us vanquish our pride. How does each of the sayings below help us all conquer our proclivity to be prideful?

Proverbs 8:13

Proverbs 11:2

Proverbs 14:3

Proverbs 16:18

18. Reread Esther 5:13 carefully. What was the main reason Haman hated Mordecai?

19. How much does God love the Jews (Romans 9:1–5)? Why?

A proud man is always looking down on things and people: and, of course, as long as you are looking down, you cannot see something that is above you.[7]
—C. S. Lewis

DIGGING DEEPER

Read Philippians 2:5–11. What do we learn about humility or "looking up" from Jesus?

DIGGING DEEPER

What is God's future plan for Israel and the Jewish people (Romans 11)? How does this reality affect your view of world affairs today?

20. What is God's ultimate desire for Jews and Gentiles (Ephesians 2:11–21)?

21. How does God feel about Christians judging those who are different (James 2:1–9), like those who are of a different race or ethnicity?

> I have given them the glory that you gave me, that they may be one as we are one—I in them and you in me—so that they may be brought to complete unity. Then the world will know that you sent me and have loved them even as you have loved me.
> —Jesus (John 17:22-23)

22. How have you struggled with the inclination to see people like you as superior? What can you do to fulfill Jesus's last prayer requests for us in John 17:22–24?

23. What did Haman's wife and friends counsel him to do (Esther 5:14)? What did Haman think of their advice?

24. Read Matthew 18:15. What does Jesus command we do first when attempting to make peace with another Christian? Why do you think Jesus insists you keep the matter "just between the two of you"?

25. When you are offended or at odds with someone, how do your closest friends react if you vent to them? Do they fuel the fire or point you to God?

None of the things that happen to you, none of the troubles you encounter, have any power to get between you and God, dilute his grace in you, divert his will from you.[8]
—Eugene Peterson

26. If our friend agrees with us while we vent, we can feel validated and then justify our foolish responses. At what point does the conversation or action turn to sin according to the Bible (Proverbs 11:13; 16:28; James 4:1–6; 2 Corinthians 12:20)?

27. Are you the kind of friend who fuels the fire or points others to God during conflict? What are some steps you could take to pause and wait on the Lord for direction with your friends during these times?

28. Read Isaiah 40:28–31 and write down everything it says about God. Considering that list and all you learned in this lesson, what can you discover about patiently waiting on God? How might that surrender impact your peace?

WISDOM IN WAITING

We live in an on-demand world.

Because of credit cards, we no longer have to save up our hard-earned cash to make a purchase. Because of curbside grocery pickup, we can bypass checkout lanes and let someone else load our wares while we relax in the comfort of our cars. Because of streaming services, we no longer have to wait for someone to return a movie we've been wanting to see (anyone else remember "Be kind, please rewind"?).

While the on-demand culture is convenient (I, Rebecca, do love me some curbside pickup), what formative effect does it have on our hearts?

God created humankind in his image, and God is not an on-demand God. In fact, the Greek word *makrothumia*, used for "patience" in the New Testament, is used in its adjective form when God describes himself to Moses: "The Lord, the Lord, the compassionate and gracious God, *slow to anger*, abounding in love and faithfulness" (Exodus 34:6). To display patience is to mirror our Father, and God's fuse is long.

Rather than rushing from one task to the next, the Lord works rhythmically, like the ebb and flow of the tide or the turning of the seasons. In stark contrast to our society's frantic pace, God. Moves. Slow.

And if you're anything like me, you don't like to wait.

In 2009, I sensed a call to ministry. At the time, I cohosted one of the most successful morning shows on the biggest country radio station in the Dallas–Fort Worth area. I loved the job, but at that point all I wanted to do was go to seminary and teach the Bible.

But God said, "Wait."

Two years later, my husband and I knew that the Lord was telling me to leave my well-paying radio gig and enter a season of study. Certain that meant seminary, I left my job, applied to Dallas Theological Seminary, and rejoiced upon my acceptance.

Still God said, "Wait."

Several years later, the Lord had led me back into broadcasting, this time at a Christian radio station. Through a series of "chance" encounters, I met several alumni and professors at DTS—one of whom agreed to mentor me (thank you, Sue!). When I finally felt God's release to reapply and enroll, the general manager at the radio station reached out to the seminary to see if they could work out a trade deal so that I could receive a tuition discount in exchange for advertising.

I could've ignored the Lord's directive to wait, and started school immediately after leaving my job. But the cost would've placed a stress on our household income (which we'd nearly cut in half). Instead, the Lord led me to seminary in a roundabout way—one that contributed to our income and blessed my family instead of burdening it.

I ultimately waited six years between my call to ministry and my formal training, but God didn't waste those years. He prepared me for the rigors of higher education in ways that I could not have foreseen. To wait patiently on the Lord displays faith and trust. And God is trustworthy. He is never hurried, never worried, and never late.

Are you in a season of waiting? Be patient, friend. God's timing always has been and always will be perfect.

Divine Providence Unfurled

LESSON 6

Looking back, God's guiding hand was evident, but at the time, the situation made absolutely no sense.

Several years after I (Sue) graduated from Dallas Theological Seminary, a friend called, alerting me to a job opening she thought I should consider—an adviser to woman students at my alma mater. My heart raced with delight at the prospect, but after reading the job description, I knew I was hopelessly underqualified. I didn't possess the credentials or the experience. But something in me wouldn't rest until I applied.

Surprisingly, the dean of students called me to come to campus for an interview. We enjoyed a lively conversation as he shared his new vision for the staff position. He desired to enrich the ethos on campus for woman students. It was in every way my ministry dream job. However, at the end, he admitted that I didn't have the doctoral degree necessary for the position. We probably both wondered why he had called me in for an interview. I walked away thinking how grand it would be to work for and learn from him and to serve there. Alas, it was not to be. I spent the next seven years leading a ministry for women at a Dallas megachurch.

I loved my time at that church, but as I sensed the Lord leading me elsewhere, the phone rang. To my astonishment, the Dallas Theological Seminary dean of students was calling and asking me to come to campus for another interview—seven years later! We met the next day, and he offered me the position on the spot. The woman with two PhDs whom they'd originally hired left under a cloud of moral failure, they'd waived the degree requirement, and suddenly I was in. My experience in the megachurch proved invaluable in my new role as adviser to woman students.

After seven years in that role and completing a doctorate, I was offered a full-time tenure-track professor position. I specialize in teaching education and women's ministry courses, which I've loved for almost twenty-five years.

OPTIONAL

Memorize Isaiah 40:22–24

He sits enthroned above the circle of the earth, and its people are like grasshoppers. He stretches out the heavens like a canopy, and spreads them out like a tent to live in. He brings princes to naught and reduces the rulers of this world to nothing. No sooner are they planted, no sooner are they sown, no sooner do they take root in the ground, than he blows on them and they wither, and a whirlwind sweeps them away like chaff.

It has been well said that "although the *name* of God is not in this book, the *hand* of God is plainly to be seen throughout." Nowhere is this more clearly manifested than in the present chapter, every verse of which attests His overruling providence and His unfailing love and care for His people, in a wrong place though they were.[1]

—H. A. Ironside

In the story of Esther God was using the ordinary events of life to realize his covenant promises to his people. He used even seemingly insignificant events, such as the king's sleepless night, and the decisions of less-than-perfect people to fulfill nevertheless the promises of his ancient covenant. . . . What a great God we serve![2]

—Karen Jobes

How foolish I felt applying for that first campus job, but it dominoed into years of fulfilling investment in the lives of hundreds of students. Only the sovereign hand of God would have worked behind the scenes this way, and I'm beyond grateful.

Trust him. When you sense him leading, follow in faith, even though sometimes his leading may not make sense. He just might be up to something wonderful!

A SERENDIPITY OF SURPRISES

Read Esther 6:1–14.

The Lord led Queen Esther to delay her request to the king and her accusation of Haman by one day. This allowed time for God's sovereign will to fall into place.

According to Esther 6:1, every official act of the Persian court was recorded in "the book of the chronicles." From these records, the king could identify and generously reward those who protected the royals from assassination plots, all too common.

1. The king *just happened* to experience insomnia the night between Esther's two banquets. What did he discover as a result (vv. 1–3)?

Momentous events often hang upon the tiniest trivialities. . . .

I love the first three words of 6:1, "During *that* night." That's the way it is with God. At the eleventh hour, He steps in. He does the unexpected. When no one seems to notice and no one seems to care, He notices and He cares.[3]

—Charles Swindoll

2. Xerxes's insomnia might seem coincidental, but God was at work. He is working quietly through circumstances in your life too. Share a time when you looked back and discerned that God had been working for your good or the good of others even though you had not recognized it at the time.

3. Some five years earlier, Mordecai had foiled an assassination plot against Xerxes but never received the public recognition typically

awarded. Surely he was disappointed, but he overlooked the insult and continued to serve the king faithfully. What do you learn about Mordecai from this response and reaction?

Although his good deed was recorded in the history books, Mordecai had gone unrewarded. But God was saving Mordecai's reward for the right time. Just as Haman was about to execute Mordecai unjustly, the king was ready to give him his reward. Although God promises to reward our good deeds, we sometimes feel our "payoff" is too far away. Be patient. God steps in when it will do the most good.[4]
—*NLT Chronological Life Application Study Bible*

4. From what you have learned so far about Haman and Mordecai, contrast them by writing (or drawing) their respective personal attributes and moral characters.

According to Herodotus (*Histories* 3.138–141), Persian kings normally honored and rewarded those who helped them immediately. For example, a man who saved the life of Xerxes' brother was immediately rewarded by being appointed the governor of Cilicia (Herodotus *Histories* 9.107).[5]
—Gary Smith

5. Why do you think so many Christians struggle with pride? Why is pride known as the "Christian's Achilles' heel"?

Pride brings a person low, but the lowly in spirit gain honor.
—Proverbs 29:23

6. Specifically, when do you tend to wrestle with pride? Why? What are some steps you could take to beat down pride and grow in humility? (See Philippians 2:2–3; 4:8–9; Colossians 3:1–4.)

7. Haman "just happened" to show up in court early that day, so the king could seek his advice on "what should be done for the man

the king delights to honor." What does Haman suggest and why (vv. 4–9)?

> The mighty Haman is rendered powerless by a "chance event" when the king just happens to have a sleepless night. He just happens to have the chronicles of his reign read to him. The story of Mordecai's loyalty just happens to come to his attention at the same moment when Haman just happens to be plotting Mordecai's death.[6]
> —Karen Jobes

8. What irony do you observe in verse 10? What do you think might have been going through Haman's mind as he obeyed the king's command?

> Synonyms for pride include arrogance, presumption, conceit, self-satisfaction, boasting, and high-mindedness. It is the opposite of humility, the proper attitude one should have in relation to God. Pride is rebellion against God because it attributes to oneself the honor and glory due to God alone.[7]
> —Gerald Cowen

9. In verse 11, Haman was to parade Mordecai through the streets of the city on the king's horse proclaiming, "This is what is done for the man the king delights to honor!" How do you think he felt as he walked beside Mordecai, shouting these words?

> God, from all eternity, did, by the most wise and holy counsel of his own will, freely, and unchangeably ordain whatsoever comes to pass.[8]
> —Westminster Confession

10. What do you think Mordecai might have been thinking and feeling about the morning's unexpected events?

DIGGING DEEPER

Look back over Esther's saga so far. Make a chart comparing Haman's pride and Mordecai's humility.

11. Can you recall a time when an unexpected blessing from God changed the direction of your life? If so, share it with the group. How has this experience affected your faith?

12. After parading Mordecai through the streets of Susa, Haman ran home to his family and advisers to rant about what happened. How did they react (v. 13)?

> The reversal dethroning Haman and empowering Mordecai shows that, despite their sin and despite their location away from Jerusalem, God's promise to Israel made at the beginning of their nation still stands. He will still destroy those who want to destroy his people, no matter where they are living. The book of Esther shows that the Jews living in the Persian empire are still under God's covenantal care.[9]
>
> —Karen Jobes

13. While Haman listened to his family's and advisers' reactions, the king's eunuchs arrived to escort him to Esther's final banquet (v. 14). If you were Haman, what emotions do you think you might feel on the way to the banquet?

MORE IRONIC REVERSALS

Read Esther 7:1–10.

Esther 7, full of intrigue, rivals the climactic scene of any Netflix drama. These words chronicle actual events that have provided a peek into God's passionate love and care for his own people. His actions are beyond our understanding, for he works in mysterious ways, often behind the curtain, to do what only God can do—orchestrate favorable outcomes when least expected.

14. Esther, Xerxes, and Haman ate and drank at Esther's second banquet (v. 1). Who would you suspect had indigestion as they dined? Why?

> Haman had wealth, but he craved something even his money couldn't buy—respect. He could buy the trappings of success and power, but his lust for popularity had become an obsession.[10]
>
> —*NLT Chronological Life Application Study Bible*

15. For the third time, the king asked Esther to reveal her request. Finally, she answered. In a nutshell, what were her two requests (v. 3)?

The reader will also notice the extensive use of the literary technique of irony. This results in reversals of what is expected. Thus, Haman's plan to destroy Mordecai ends up destroying himself. The sharpened pole built for Mordecai is used to kill Haman. Haman's decree allowed for people to take the wealth of the Jews, but in actuality Haman's wealth ends up in Jewish hands. Mordecai ends up with Haman's job. Haman wanted someone to glorify him on the king's horse, but he is instead commanded to glorify Mordecai, who rides on the king's horse.[11]

—Gary Smith

I have seen a wicked and ruthless man flourishing like a luxuriant native tree, but he soon passed away and was no more; though I looked for him, he could not be found

—David (Psalm 37:35-36)

DIGGING DEEPER

Recall a biblical figure who exhibited similar attributes as Haman. What was their final demise? What lessons can we learn from the life of Haman?

The story of Esther concerns deliverance for the Jews during *exile* years. The book does not intend to extol the Jew, but to show that the fate of the nation—good or bad—is in the hands of a sovereign God. There have been tragic pogroms [massacres] in the history of Israel, but there have also been miraculous deliverances, and the book of Esther records one such deliverance.[12]

—Irving Jensen

16. Why were Esther and all the Jews in Persia in danger of annihilation (v. 4)?

17. Review the original decree in Esther 3:8–9. What had Haman failed to mention to the king in the decree? How had the king responded to Haman's request regarding this decree (3:10–11)?

18. According to Esther 1:19, Persian decrees could not be annulled (see also Daniel 6:8). Why might this reality have made this situation awkward for Xerxes?

19. When the king exclaimed, "Who is he? Where is he—the man who has dared to do such a thing?" what did Esther reveal (vv. 5–6)?

20. Why do you think the king immediately left to go outside to the palace garden (v. 7)?

21. Why do you think Haman fell on Esther's couch? How did the king react to the scene when he returned from the garden? Why? (vv. 7–8)

Persian etiquette required that no man, except the king, ever be left alone, touch, or come within seven feet of a woman in his harem, especially the queen.[13]

22. What did the king's eunuch explain to Xerxes? How did the king react and what did he command them to do? (vv. 9–10)

The Persians, Greeks, and Romans would cover the face of someone found guilty of a crime. This practice still exists in some executions today.[14]

23. Why do you think the king was outraged by the whole situation? Was he justified? Why or why not?

In a universe in which the sovereign God accomplishes his will by his meticulous providence, nothing happens by chance. There are no coincidences. Luck and sovereignty don't mix.[15]
—Tony Evans

24. List what had happened on this day at this point that would ultimately bring about the deliverance of the Jews and the preservation of their line. What might have been the long-term consequences if Esther had not succeeded?

You intended to harm me, but God intended it for good to accomplish what is now being done, the saving of many lives.
—Joseph (Genesis 50:20)

25. What have you learned in this lesson about God and his abilities? How might these truths affect your life today?

In the LORD's hand the king's heart is a stream of water that he channels toward all who please him.
—Proverbs 21:1

“Surely the day is coming; it will burn like a furnace. All the arrogant and every evildoer will be stubble, and the day that is coming will set them on fire,” says the LORD Almighty. “Not a root or a branch will be left to them. But for you who revere my name, the sun of righteousness will rise with healing in its rays. And you will go out and frolic like well-fed calves. Then you will trample on the wicked; they will be ashes under the soles of your feet on the day when I act,” says the LORD Almighty.
—Malachi 4:1-3

GOSPEL SEEDLINGS IN ESTHER'S STORY

It sat in my (Rebecca's) pantry for years—ten? Twelve? Maybe even fifteen. I received the Chia Pet (remember those?) at a white elephant Christmas party and promptly forgot about it until my husband and I decided to spring-clean the kitchen. He pulled the box out from under the bottom shelf, wiped off a thick layer of dust, and exclaimed, “What in the world is this?”

“Oh my goodness,” I replied. “We got that at one of your aunt's Christmas parties, remember?” Shaking his head, he put it in the throw-away pile. A few minutes later, our daughter wandered into the kitchen and picked it up. Thinking it would be a fun project for the kids, I decided to keep it and see if we could get the seeds to sprout.

A look at the label dashed my hopes. It was almost ten years past the expiration date, but at my kids' insistence, we set it on a window, watered it according to the directions, and sat back to wait.

We didn't have to wait long. Tiny green sprouts poked through the terra-cotta hedgehog within a few days, and two weeks later, “Harry the Hedgehog” had a thick green coat. It turns out that Chia seeds, when stored in a cool, dark place, can sit dormant longer than the Chia Pet label belied.

In the next chapter of Esther, we will see that Haman's failed attempt to assassinate the Jews created fertile ground for seeds of faith to take root and grow. The author writes, “Many from the peoples of the country declared themselves Jews, for fear of the Jews had fallen on them” (8:17 ESV).

We see nearly identical language in Joshua 2:9 when Rahab hid the spies because “the fear of you [the Israelites] has fallen upon us” (ESV). Rahab and her family aligned themselves with Israel (and Israel's God) because they knew only God could deliver the Jews from the hands of the Egyptians. God's fame had spread among the Canaanites. By the first century AD, pockets of Jews and God-fearers (Gentiles who worshipped God) were dispersed across the Roman Empire—including the former Persian territory. They met weekly in synagogues to worship, pray, and listen to the Scriptures.

Today we know that these groups of people were among the first to accept the message of Christ and were largely responsible for the gospel's rapid spread. Not only did God sovereignly foil Haman's attempted genocide, but he also used Haman to plant the seeds that would someday grow into the church as we know it.

Two lessons to go as Esther's saga culminates into a piece of history. Be sure to designate quality time to spend in God's Word and finish well.

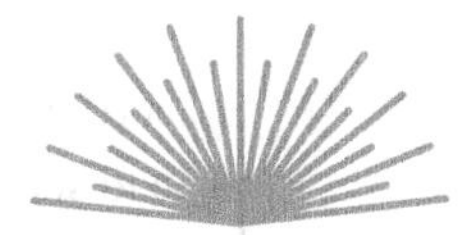

Divine Providence Fulfilled

LESSON 7

The American colonists had endured Great Britain's taxation without representation long enough. The time had come to declare their independence. On June 11, 1776, Thomas Jefferson sequestered himself in a rented room at a boarding house in Philadelphia, vowing not to emerge without a document in hand. Less than three weeks later, he presented his first draft of America's Declaration of Independence to the members of Congress. On July 2, 1776, the delegates voted to sever all ties with King George III.

The Revolutionary War, however, raged on. Refusing to surrender, British General Charles Cornwallis marched his troops from North Carolina to Virginia, waiting for British naval forces to arrive with reinforcements. But the French, who had allied themselves with the American colonists, thwarted the British ships, enabling George Washington to ambush Cornwallis's men in Yorktown. The British retreated, and on September 3, 1783, American leaders met with British representatives in France to sign the Treaty of Paris. The Revolutionary War was over.

As we open our Bibles to Esther 8, we feel the tension that America's Founding Fathers must have felt. The Declaration of Independence had been issued and signed. But their enemies remained at large. In much the same way, King Xerxes had executed evil Haman, but the threat of annihilation still hovered over the Jews like storm clouds pregnant with rain.

How would God orchestrate saving the Jews from extinction when an order to the contrary still circulated throughout the land, specifying a day when the enemies of the Jews could freely kill them without any legal consequences? Stay tuned to find out.

Earlier in the day, as we saw in chapter 7, Queen Esther had succeeded in tearing off Haman's evil mask, unveiling his plot to kill the Jews. Later that same day, Xerxes found Haman inappropriately fawning over Esther on her couch, hoping she would take pity on him and spare his life. This

OPTIONAL

Memorize 1 Peter 5:5–7

All of you, clothe yourselves with humility toward one another, because, "God opposes the proud but shows favor to the humble." Humble yourselves, therefore, under God's mighty hand, that he may lift you up in due time. Cast all your anxiety on him because he cares for you.

action so enraged Xerxes that he ordered Haman impaled on the pole he had set up for Mordecai.

MORDECAI'S RISE TO POWER

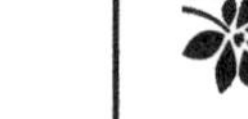

Read Esther 8:1–2.

1. What did Xerxes do next (v. 1)? What did Esther do with her new property (v. 2)? What would this mean for Mordecai?

According to ancient historian Josephus, often the state would confiscate the property of an enemy.[1]

The king has saved Esther's life along with the life of her family, and he has given Mordecai a powerful position; so the king assumes that will be enough for Esther. The king assumes that Esther will be satisfied with having her own life spared and having the only family she knows elevated to power. He assumes Esther will be able to forget about the fate of the rest of the Jews and simply return to living for herself. He assumes that, because that is exactly what he intends to do.[2]
—Timothy Cain

2. What else did Xerxes do to honor Mordecai (v. 2)?

3. Who had possessed the signet ring before Mordecai? How had this person used the ring in the past? What kind of power was now available to Mordecai? (3:10–12)

In a world of honor and shame, justice can only occur when honor is restored. Honor can only be restored with the death of the enemy. The threat to Jewish lives that came with the shame must be vindicated. Since Haman shamed the Jews, he in turn needed to be shamed—and he was: impaled on a pole, without honor.[3]
—Peter Lau

4. Glance back at 7:3. What did Esther ask of the king again? How much of her request had he granted at this point?

THE THREAT REMAINS

Read Esther 8:3–17.

Haman was dead, but the threat to the Jews remained firmly intact. After an undetermined period of time, Esther visited the king once more.

5. Why were the Jews still in danger? (See 1:19 for a reminder about Persian laws.)

In these last lessons we have watched the movements of various characters in the book of Esther. However, whoever the character, the hand of God was behind the scenes. The destinies of God's creatures are all part of a divine design, known fully to God alone. If chance determined those destinies, the world would have destroyed itself long ago.[4]
—Irving Jensen

6. What did Esther risk by approaching the king again (4:11)? How has she matured since Mordecai first asked her to intercede for the Jews?

Although spiritual growth is generally a process, I (Sue) have found that I've grown exponentially after times when I've stepped outside my comfort zone or been forced to face situations where I've had to trust God more—for example, prison ministry, mission trips, conflicts, leading a new ministry, and speaking before a new crowd. But after facing these kinds of challenges and witnessing God's supernatural strength, I come out on the other side more resolute, more courageous, and more grateful for God's amazing enablement. I wonder if Esther's recent traumatic ordeal did the same for her.

7. Recall a time when you went through a season of spiritual growth. When was it? What were the circumstances? What did you learn?

8. Reread 8:3. What did Esther do next? Why?

Unwittingly victimized by an unbearable situation, she [Esther] stepped up and determined, by God's grace, to make a difference. Throwing protocol to the wind and ignoring all her fears, this woman stood in a gap most of her peers would never have risked. In doing so, she not only exposed and foiled the plans of an evil man, who, like Adolph Hitler, had a violent agenda. She alone saved her nation from extermination. Now, that's what I call *power*![5]
—Charles Swindoll

Just as Xerxes king of Persia could not simply rescind the first decree of death, God, King of the universe, cannot simply rescind the decree of death pronounced in the garden of Eden against humanity. Instead, he issues a counter-decree of life, the gospel of Jesus Christ.[6]
—Karen Jobes and Janet Nygren

When you mix the power of an awesome God with the power of a godly woman, you've got a winning combination.[8]
—Charles Swindoll

Chapter 8 is a chapter of reversals, and will replay, with significant changes, some of the motifs and actions from earlier in the story.[9]
—Adele Berlin

9. Esther's plea in verse 5 echoes her words to the king in 7:3. How are they similar? What has Esther added? Why the increased intensity?

10. Have you ever found yourself completely at the mercy of someone else? If so, describe the situation. How did you feel?

Esther navigated a delicate situation wisely. She knew she needed to avoid shaming the king or assigning responsibility to him for the plight of the Jews. Mervin Breneman points out, "Esther did not use the word 'law,' for she knew that Persian laws could not be repealed. She put all the blame on Haman and avoided blaming the king."[7]

11. To avoid needlessly shaming someone is to extend Christ's kindness. Have you ever been in a situation where someone helped you save face? What happened? How did you feel?

12. Perhaps you were the one who graciously saved someone from embarrassment over a mistake they made. Describe the circumstances. Why did you spare them shame?

13. How did Xerxes respond to Esther's request (vv. 7–8)?

14. Reread the king's response to Haman in 3:10–11. How is this earlier reply similar to Xerxes's answer to Esther? What does this tell us about Xerxes's problem-solving ability? Had the embarrassment over his dealings with Haman changed him in any way?

15. Compare Haman's decree (3:12–15) to Mordecai's (8:9–17) in the chart below.

	HAMAN	MORDECAI
What did the secretaries write out (3:12; 8:9)?	An edict written in the name of the king	An edict written in the name of the king
Who were the orders addressed to (3:12; 8:9)?		
What did the orders say (3:13; 8:11)?		
When was the order to be carried out (3:13; 8:12)?		
How did the people respond (3:15; 8:15–17)?		

DIGGING DEEPER

List as many reversals as you can in the story of Esther so far, noting the chapters and verses. What does this teach you about God? How does this point us to Christ?

Note the differences in the two edicts.

This time, the edict was also sent in the Jews' language.

Haman's edict was about the Jews' destruction. Mordecai's edict was about the Jews' salvation. Haman's edict caused confusion; Mordecai's caused rejoicing.

In Haman's edict, the king *decreed* the annihilation of the Jews. In Mordecai's edict, the king *allowed* the Jews to protect themselves.

Law and justice may be the public ideal of every great government, but people in power, compelled by their own fears and anxieties, all too often abuse the power with which they have been entrusted. Absolute power held by flawed leaders is a terrifying scenario. . . .

Only a king with perfect character is worthy of absolute power.[10]

—Karen Jobes

16. From these differences, what observations can you make about the way God works?

17. Paul, writing under the influence of the Holy Spirit, said to the Galatians, "Don't be misled—you cannot mock the justice of God. You will always harvest what you plant" (Galatians 6:7 NLT). How did that principle manifest itself in Haman's life and the lives of his followers?

I [The LORD] will bless those who bless you, and whoever curses you I will curse; and all peoples on earth will be blessed through you.

—Genesis 12:3

18. Clarity is kindness. The people living in Susa, Jews and Gentiles alike, had now received two conflicting orders written in the king's name. The first one, which was associated with Haman, ordered the Jews' extinction. The second one, which was associated with Mordecai, gave the Jews permission to fight back. How must the Gentiles living in the region have felt upon receiving the opposing commands from their king? Have you ever been the recipient of mixed messages? What were the circumstances? How did you handle the situation?

Throughout the book, the author contrasts the forthright, bold, sacrificial, and honest behavior of Esther and Mordecai with the angry, arrogant, and inappropriate behavior of the king and Haman.[11]

—Gary Smith

God never sends mixed messages. From Genesis to Revelation, we observe that God is a God of order, not chaos. But ever since the fall of Adam and Eve, chaos has invaded every aspect of life—nature, work, home, and relationships. The story of Esther shows us that even when it looks like nothing is happening, God is working behind the scenes to speak order into chaos.

> We are to live with the knowledge that both our best moments and our worst are all a part of what God is doing in us and through us in the lives of others. We cannot see the end of the matter from the beginning or the middle. The story of Esther assures us that we do not have to.[12]
>
> —Karen Jobes

19. Where are you experiencing chaos right now? What steps could you take to help the situation? Write a prayer asking God to speak order into your circumstances.

> Neither Mordecai nor Esther retreated into a cloistered life to avoid people who had different political and theological beliefs. Instead, they entered the fray and lived by their own beliefs and standards of conduct.[13]
>
> —Gary Smith

20. Explain how you think Mordecai's new decree might have influenced the Jews' faith. How does it affect yours?

21. The Jews were not the only people impacted by the new decree. Reread 8:17 and fill in the blanks.

    In every province and in every city to which the edict of the king came, there was joy and gladness among the Jews, with feasting and celebrating. And many people of other ________________ became __________ because __________ of the Jews had seized them.

God orchestrates a variety of situations to woo unbelievers to trust him. In this case, he used healthy fear. What other methods have you observed God using to draw unbelievers to faith?

DIGGING DEEPER

The Psalms and the book of Isaiah were written hundreds of years before the events in Esther. Read Psalm 30 and Isaiah 61. How do these passages reflect the sentiments of the Jews in 8:15–17?

22. Read Genesis 12:3. What is one of God's purposes for humankind? How did the Jews in Persia illustrate this purpose?

23. Specifically, how can God use you to bless others right now? What initial steps do you need to take to make this blessing a reality?

24. Like Esther and the Jews in Persia, have you experienced a painful situation that God has redeemed and woven into your story? Write it out, and if you feel comfortable, share it to bless others in your group.

CLOTHES SPEAK

Clothes often serve as literary clues in the Bible. Joseph's "Technicolor dreamcoat" represented more than fine fashion; it signified his position as the favored child to his brothers and that their father, Jacob, had selected him to receive the blessing typically reserved for the firstborn son (in this case, Reuben).[15] David's daughter Tamar tore her long robe with sleeves, typical attire for the king's unwed daughters, and covered her head with ashes to display her deep grief after her brother Amnon raped her (2 Samuel 13:19).

Mordecai's wardrobe change also carries literary significance. The author introduces Mordecai as a man of honor. First, we see that he had taken in his orphaned relative and raised her as his daughter (Esther 2:7). Next, he foiled the officers' plot to assassinate Xerxes (v. 22), an act tradi-

DIGGING DEEPER

In Esther 8:17, we hear echoes of Rahab's response to the Jewish spies sent to scout out Jericho. Read Joshua 2:8–11 and note places where you see parallels. In addition to saving the Jews scattered throughout the Persian Empire, what do you think God might have wanted the Persians to learn about himself (see Joshua 2:11)?

See the relationship of the truths communicated in the story of Esther to the everyday reality of your own life. One way to do this is to realize that the gallows you think are prepared for you are not that at all.

What might those looming gallows be? Some horrible pain? Some threat of illness or need for surgery? Some emotional stress that is leading to what appears to be your emotional demise? Some fractured relationship that you cannot repair or get beyond? . . .

. . . *Stop all that!* . . .

. . . Say to the Lord God, "I am *convinced* that You are at work amid the gallows of my life."[14]

—Charles Swindoll

DIGGING DEEPER

Although God remained conspicuously silent in the book of Esther, he ultimately used the Jews' circumstances to point to his salvific work. Can you think of other biblical persons who endured hardship so that God might be glorified? Who? How? (For examples, see 2 Corinthians 11:22–29 and Acts 7:54–60.)

tionally richly rewarded by Persian kings who feared for their lives. To the readers' astonishment, however, it was Haman who was singled out and promoted to a position of honor. Such positions, by the way, were typically accompanied by a change in attire.

Haman received the homage—and the robe—due to Mordecai.

The narrator again highlights Mordecai's garments when the royal edict decreeing the Jews' destruction goes out. Chapter 4 opens with Mordecai tearing his clothes and putting on sackcloth and ashes (v. 1). Esther responded by sending her father figure a change of—you guessed it—clothes. When the king asked Haman what he should do for "the man the king delights to honor," Haman promptly replied, "Have them bring a royal robe the king has worn and a horse the king has ridden, one with a royal crest placed on its head" (6:7–8). And in a royal reversal, Mordecai wore the robe Haman thought would be his.

Chapter 8 concludes with yet another nod to Mordecai's duds. The author writes, "When Mordecai left the king's presence, he was wearing royal garments of blue and white, a large crown of gold and a purple robe of fine linen. And the city of Susa held a joyous celebration" (v. 15).

Across the narrative of Esther, the author moves Mordecai from rags of grief to royal splendor. But might there be more? The description of Mordecai's robes also echoes descriptions of the garments made for the priests who would minister in the tabernacle (Exodus 39:1; Leviticus 8:9). The priests mediated between the Israelites and God, representing God to the people and the people to God.

Dressed in royal garb with the king's signet ring on his finger, Mordecai stood in the image and likeness of the king himself. But he (and Esther!) also acted as priests—interceding for the people and carrying their concerns to the Lord. Together, Queen Esther and Mordecai point us to the King of Kings and our great High Priest, who laid down his life for his people to once and for all conquer the enemy of the Jews and the world.

And by the way, when Christ returns for his bride, the church, we'll all receive a brand-new change of clothes too (Isaiah 61:10; Revelation 19:8).

Divine Providence Celebrated

LESSON 8

As my husband and I (Sue) pulled into the garage, our terrified sixteen-year-old daughter burst through the back door and fell into my arms. Heather, exhausted from her first day as a hospital volunteer, had decided to stay home while the rest of the family engaged in our first boating lesson. Tucked cozily in her bed and fast asleep, she had awoken to the sound of men's voices and someone breaking down the back door.

She sent up a flare prayer, and the Lord led her to feign sleep rather than confront the intruders. She realized a 105-pound teenage girl had little chance of fighting off a group of male marauders. They rustled through the house, packing up electronics and other items of value. Then silence. Were they gone?

No. She distinctly remembers one peering into her bedroom and murmuring something to the others. Her heart pounding out of her chest, she had squinched her eyes tight and prayed. More whispering, followed by silence. She lay there for what she said seemed like an hour, anxiously anticipating the garage door lifting and our car pulling in. The police conjectured that, upon seeing her in the house, the thieves sprinted out the front door with their plunder, forgetting to close it on the way out. But what if they hadn't left? After the police assessed the scene and we all calmed down, I slept on the floor next to Heather's bed that night.

Thankfully, she rebounded quickly and didn't suffer traumatic repercussions from the experience. Having come to faith as a small child, she accepted that God had protected her for a reason, and inheriting her father's even temperament didn't hurt either.

However, this experience raised a series of questions in our family's minds. When perilous situations occur, what would God have us do? If someone wants to hurt us, can we defend ourselves? How does the Lord want us to respond when danger threatens our lives or the lives of loved

OPTIONAL

Memorize Psalm 70:1–2

Hasten, O God, to save me; come quickly, LORD, to help me. May those who want to take my life be put to shame and confusion; may all who desire my ruin be turned back in disgrace.

ones? And how is that different from seeking revenge against people who offend us or offend those we love?

Esther and the Jews in Persia found themselves in this situation. They even knew the exact day their enemies had license to murder them. What would you have done?

This final lesson will help us answer these important questions, especially as the persecution of Christians becomes more prevalent.

The biblical authors do not prohibit self-defense. Neither, however, do they insist on it. Believers must rely on the Holy Spirit, who gives wisdom generously to all who ask (James 1:5). Solomon writes that there is a time for everything, for love and hate, war and peace (Ecclesiastes 3:1, 8). This means we must discern when to rise up in defense and when to turn the other cheek (Matthew 5:39).

Before we continue Esther's story, let's investigate what the Bible says about justified self-defense, first in the Old Testament law and then in the New Testament. Remember that Christians today are not bound by the Mosaic law. Jesus instigated a new covenant (Luke 22:20) and a new era—the church age. However, we can glean general principles from the Mosaic law to help us live holy lives.

1. Read Exodus 21:22–25 and Leviticus 24:17–22. In each passage, what are the situations, and what is the penalty set forth in the Mosaic law? What general principles do these two texts teach you about justice, retribution, and the value of human life?

2. Jesus referenced the Mosaic law in the Sermon on the Mount. Read Matthew 5:38–42. Compare Jesus's teachings with the passages you read in Exodus and Leviticus. How are they different? How are they the same?

3. New Testament authors Paul and Peter reference Jesus's Sermon on the Mount. Dissect the verses below and discuss their implications for how we deal with people who offend us. What about those who desire to harm us physically? Do any of these New Testament principles deal with murder or grievous bodily harm?

1 Peter 3:9–12

Romans 12:17–21

One reason the Nazis hated the Jews so much was that the Jews represented God to them. The Bible—including its writers, its holidays, its prophets, its Messiah—were Jewish.[1]
—John Bisagno

4. Reread Romans 12:20. How might showing unmerited kindness bring about positive change in our enemies? (See also Proverbs 25:21–22.) Who in your life might soften and repent if you take this approach?

5. Have you ever let your anger smolder to the extent that you wanted to retaliate? How did Jesus advise his disciples when they asked about forgiving those who had wronged them (Matthew 6:12, 14–15; 18:21–22)?

"In your anger do not sin": Do not let the sun go down while you are still angry, and do not give the devil a foothold.
—The apostle Paul (Ephesians 4:26–27)

6. How did Paul advise Christians to treat fellow believers who sinned against them (Colossians 3:12–14)?

DIGGING DEEPER

Summarize what you have learned about God's direction for Christians related to justified self-defense versus revenge.

That's like giving concentration camp prisoners long-overdue rights. It's cutting the barbed wires. It's feeding *them* rather than the guards. It's an unlimited, no-holds-barred edict.[2]
—Charles Swindoll

Now, let's rejoin Esther's story. The lives of Persian Jews were being threatened. Two edicts had been issued. The first, authored by Haman, allowed anyone to kill their Jewish neighbors on a particular day. Since Persian edicts could not be rescinded, Mordecai wrote a second mandate. It granted Jews the right to assemble, protect themselves and their loved ones, and confiscate all their enemies' possessions on that dreaded day.

Esther 9:5 states that the Jews "did what they pleased to those who hated them." This might be misconstrued as indiscriminate murder, but many commentators don't think so. They take it to mean that the Jews' defensive actions were well within the king's retributive allowance.

Read Esther 9:1–10.

7. Many Persian hearts had been corrupted by anti-Semitic hatred. What had they planned to do on that day? What happened instead? (v. 1)

8. How did the Jews protect themselves from the Persians bent on killing them (vv. 2, 5)?

Then, one day, the tables are turned. The enormous cat becomes the mouse. The prisoner gets the gun. The victim gains the upper hand. This provides the opportunity to get even. And if there is nothing to stop him, watch out! The offended retaliates against the offender with full-scale vengeance.[3]
—Charles Swindoll

9. Specifically, who did the Jews kill, and who did they spare (vv. 6–10, 12, 15)? What does this reveal about the Jews?

DIGGING DEEPER

In Genesis 14, the author describes Abram rescuing his nephew Lot. What happened when Abram met Melchizedek, king of Salem? How did this set a precedent for how the Jews believed God wanted them to carry out future holy wars (vv. 22–24)?

10. Many Persians had been preparing for Jewish genocide for almost a year. What political strategy did God ordain to help the Jews overpower them (vv. 2–4)?

11. In verses 7–10, we see that certain Jews purposely assassinated Haman's ten sons. Why do you think they felt this was necessary?

12. Verse 10 ends by informing us that the Jews did not seize the property of the men they killed even though the edict said they could (8:11). Why do you think they refused? What does this tell you about their character?

Read Esther 9:11–19.

13. After reports came in concerning casualties on the dreaded day, the king asked Esther if she desired any additional favors (v. 12). What were her two requests (v. 13)?

14. Why do you think Esther requested a second day of fighting? Does this change your opinion of her? If so, how?

In 9:2, "no one could stand against them" does not mean that no one attacked the Jews or that the Jews suffered no casualties. It simply means that no one launched a successful barrage against them at that time. Gary Smith contends that the Jews' adversaries weren't afraid of God but instead were fearful of Mordecai and his governmental power.[4]

This is what the LORD, the God of Israel, says . . . "The days are coming," declares the LORD, "when I will bring my people Israel and Judah back from captivity and restore them to the land I gave their ancestors to possess," says the LORD.
—Jeremiah 30:2–3

DIGGING DEEPER

Read Ezra's prayer in Ezra 9:6–9. Why was he thankful? What do you learn about the state of the Jewish people at that time?

One of the rules of ancient holy war was that plunder must not be taken. When Abram, for example, fought for Sodom because his nephew Lot had been taken captive, the king of Sodom offered him material reward. Abram, however, would accept nothing, lest that wicked city be the source of his prosperity (Gen. 14). This example set a precedent for God's people.

. . . There was to be no personal profit in holy war because the destroyers were acting not on their own behalf but as agents of God's wrath.[5]
—Karen Jobes

The late first-century Jewish historian Josephus writes that seventy-five thousand Persians were killed on those two dreaded days.[6] However, Gary Smith writes that because the word for "thousands" can also be translated as "families," it might be that the Jews only killed seventy-five clans or extended families.[7]

This man [the king] relies on and respects the counsel of his wife, Esther. He's still the king. But it is obvious that her opinion matters a great deal to him. Her inner strength had been wonderfully displayed in previous hours—the way she handled her concern regarding Haman's wicked plan, the manner in which she expressed compassion for her people, the wisdom shown in her timing of silence as well as speech.[8]
—Charles Swindoll

Whether or not Esther was justified in extending the killing a second day, the perennial failure of Israel's greatest leaders to war against moral and spiritual darkness without engaging in sin themselves suggests that no one is worthy to wage true holy war in God's name. God's strategy against sin and evil was awaiting the perfect warrior, who could execute divine justice with clean hands and a pure heart. His name is Jesus.[9]
—Karen Jobes

After these two exhausting days of defending themselves, the Jews experienced tremendous relief. As a result, they rested and feasted. This celebration became known as Purim. Verses 17–19 reveal that Purim happened at different times in different places because the fighting concluded at different times in different places.

The book of Esther brings up several challenges for believers today. Distinguishing between justified self-defense, legal justice, and revenge or retaliation can be confusing. These definitions may help:

- **Justified self-defense** allows someone to use reasonable force to protect themselves or others from an imminent threat of physical harm.
- **Legal justice** is exercised by governments to establish order, punish evil, and promote justice.
- **Revenge or retaliation** is deliberately inflicting pain or injury on someone in return for an offense that that person inflicted on them or someone they care about.

15. What did God say about taking revenge or retaliating in Deuteronomy 32:35 and Romans 12:19? How is self-defense different from revenge (Exodus 22:2)?

THE TRIUMPH OF THE JEWS

Read Esther 9:20–10:3.

Every year in February or March, Jews still set aside two days to celebrate Purim. The Hebrew word *purim* literally means "lots." The name of this festival derives from the lots cast by Haman when he was trying to determine what date to carry out his plot to exterminate the Jews. Today, typical Purim festivities include reading the book of Esther, dressing up in costumes and performing the story, using noisemakers whenever Haman's name is mentioned, eating hat-shaped cookies called hamantaschen, and giving gifts to family, friends, and the poor. As the book of Esther closes, we learn more about the establishment of Purim.

16. What did Mordecai do in verse 20?

17. Why did he write to the Jews (vv. 21–22)?

18. Reread verses 27 and 28. What did the Jews do in response? List each action.

19. For thousands of years, people have set aside days of remembrance to commemorate important events or people. What are some ways that Christians do this today? Why is this an important practice?

Esther 9:22 says, "The Jews *got relief* from their enemies" (emphasis added). The verb translated "got relief" is the Hebrew word *nuach.* The author of Esther is giving us a subtle hint that God's providential hand was at work. The verb *nuach* appears in other key biblical texts describing God providing rest.

> Exodus 33:14—The Lord replied, "My Presence will go with you, and I will give you rest [*nuach*]."

The Levitical law admonished God's people to execute fair justice. But retribution was limited: "eye for eye, tooth for tooth" (Leviticus 24:20). The purpose of the law was to ensure that the punishment fit the crime. In other words, the law kept a wronged individual from exacting disproportionately harmful retribution upon another person in an act of uninhibited revenge. But the law involved the legal system and was not the primary guide in personal relationships. Why should a believer turn the other cheek? Because Christians are asked to follow the way of Christ, not the world. As he faced crucifixion, Jesus offered radical forgiveness, through the cross for the salvation of many, rather than calling down "twelve legions of angels" to inflict revenge (Matthew 26:53).

For without the royal favor of the Jews that he [Mordecai] through Esther induced, there may have been no return of Jewish exiles to Jerusalem under Ezra and Nehemiah.[10]

—Irving Jensen

DIGGING DEEPER

Study the Song of Moses in Deuteronomy 32:1–43. What do you learn about God's love for his people, Israel, and his attributes? What parts of the song do you find helpful as you navigate this fallen world today?

Deuteronomy 12:10—You will cross the Jordan and settle in the land the LORD your God is giving you as an inheritance, and he will give you rest [*nuach*] from all your enemies around you so that you will live in safety.

Joshua 21:44—The LORD gave them rest [*nuach*] on every side, just as he had sworn to their ancestors. Not one of their enemies withstood them; the LORD gave all their enemies into their hands.

20. From the three verses above, who were the ones receiving rest? Who was giving rest?

21. What did Jesus promise his followers in Matthew 11:28–30? Are you in need of rest right now? From this passage, what do you need to do to experience this rest?

22. Why did the king elevate Mordecai (10:3)? Do you "work for the good" of your people? Have you ever spoken up for their welfare? If so, how?

He [God] doesn't sit for a pen portrait in the story of Esther, but His mind, His will, His power, and His presence are working in concert on every page.[11]
—Charles Swindoll

DIGGING DEEPER

Study Joshua 3 and 4. What happened and how did God instruct the Jews to memorialize the occasion? What principles can you glean to help you celebrate your faith?

Our hurried, stressful, busy lives are unquestionably the most dangerous enemy of celebrating life itself. Somehow, we must learn how to achieve momentary slowdowns, and request from God a heightened awareness of the conception that life is a happy thing, a festival to be enjoyed rather than a drudgery to be endured.[12]
—Luci Swindoll

DIGGING DEEPER

God commanded that the Israelites commemorate various experiences with a festival. Make a chart of the mandated festivals and God's instructions on how to celebrate them (Leviticus 23; Exodus 5:1; 12:15–20; 23:14–19; 34:18–26). What do you learn to help you celebrate what God has done in your life?

23. Think back over these eight lessons. How are Esther and Mordecai models for Christians today?

24. What truths will you take away from your study of Esther? How has your faith been strengthened by working your way through her saga? What have you learned about the character of God and his love for his people?

DIGGING DEEPER

Hebrews 4:1–11 describes a future rest for faithful Christians. Does this passage infer that a Christian can lose their salvation if they disobey? If not, since that idea conflicts with other passages, what is the author teaching? For insight, consider studying the book of Hebrews with our Discover Together Bible Study guide, *Hebrews: Discovering a Better Fulfillment in Jesus* (Kregel, 2025).

The threat against the Jews of Persia was a threat against God's plan of redemption.[13]
—Karen Jobes

The life of Esther demonstrates that God can use women in powerful ways to change the course of history. . . . With the backing of a praying community of supporters, she accepted a difficult role and put her life on the line to save the Jews from genocide.[15]
—Gary Smith

ESTHER'S MANTRA: "HATE WON'T WIN"

On June 17, 2015, Dylann Roof walked in the side door of the historic Emanuel AME Church in downtown Charleston, South Carolina.[14] This twenty-one-year-old white supremacist asked to meet with the pastor, who welcomed him to join her and others in the congregation for Bible study. For the next forty minutes, Roof participated in the group discussion, occasionally disagreeing about Scripture with the other group members. When the class bowed their heads to pray, Roof took out a .45 caliber handgun and shot over seventy-five rounds, reloading seven times. He stood over his victims, shouting racial slurs and firing repeatedly. The massacre lasted approximately six minutes. Nine people died. One was hospitalized with injuries. All were Black.

Two days after this horrifying mass shooting, Roof appeared in court, where some relatives of the victims addressed him directly. Many said they were praying for his soul and offered him forgiveness. Their responses shocked the nation and garnered the media's attention.

The grandson of one of the victims began his court statement by telling Roof, "I understand why you don't want to look at us, so I will speak to the spirit that possesses you." He urged the defendant to "look at the love this nation, this holy city has poured out. You don't have to look at me.

But I see that spirit. I want you to think about that as I forgive [you] . . . for your actions. . . . Know you have an opportunity to ask for forgiveness. Know that God will forgive you. . . . If you choose to serve him, you will have a better life. I hear you breathing all the way over here. Speak to that spirit that's inside you."[16] Another grandson called on Roof to "Repent. Confess. Give your life to the one who matters the most, Christ, so he can change your ways no matter what happens to you and you'll be OK."[17]

Roof has continually insisted, "I do not regret what I did."[18] The judge sentenced him to death, and he currently awaits execution in a federal prison. He confessed that he intended to start a race war by sowing hatred and discord, but he actually achieved the opposite. For example, the Confederate flag, which had been displayed outside the South Carolina Capitol since the one-hundredth anniversary of the Civil War, was taken down after Roof's massacre. Roof had been photographed with the flag to symbolize his allegiance to white supremacy. To many, the flag signifies racist imagery. Thousands cheered when it was removed.

The granddaughter of one of the murdered pastors declared, "Hate won't win."[19] Her words perfectly capture the theme of the book of Esther and, indeed, the Bible itself. Because Jesus lives, hate won't win.

Notes

How to Get the Most out of a Discover Together Bible Study

1. Howard G. Hendricks and William D. Hendricks, *Living by the Book: The Art and Science of Reading the Bible* (Moody, 2007), 23.

Why Study Esther?

1. See section 24 of "Of God's Word" in *The Table Talk of Martin Luther*, trans. and ed. William Hazlitt (Bell and Daldy, 1872), https://ia801300.us.archive.org/20/items/cu31924029255184/cu31924029255184.pdf.

Lesson 1: Divine Providence Set in Motion

1. Charles R. Swindoll, *Esther: A Woman of Strength and Dignity* (Nelson, 1997), 3–4.
2. Karen H. Jobes, *Esther*, NIV Application Commentary (Zondervan, 1999), 38.
3. Swindoll, *Esther*, 24.
4. Jobes, *Esther*, 61.
5. Plutarch, "Advice to the Bride and Groom" section 16, trans. Donald Russell, in *Plutarch's* Advice to the Bride and Groom *and* A Consolation to His Wife*: English Translations, Commentary, Interpretive Essays, and Bibliography*, ed. Sarah B. Pomeroy (Oxford University Press, 1999), 7.
6. Swindoll, *Esther*, 30.
7. Jobes, *Esther*, 90.
8. Jobes, *Esther*, 43.
9. Jobes, *Esther*, 38.
10. Jobes, *Esther*, 41.
11. Jobes, *Esther*, 76.

Lesson 2: Divine Providence Through Pagan Rulers

1. H. A. Ironside, *Ezra, Nehemiah, and Esther*, Ironside Expository Commentary (Kregel, 2008), 154.
2. Rose Scott, "What Political Standpoint Aligns the Best with Christianity?" Quora, March 25, 2019, https://www.quora.com/What-political-standpoint-aligns-the-best-with-Christianity.
3. Charles R. Swindoll, *Esther: A Woman of Strength and Dignity* (Nelson, 1997), 34.

4. Karen H. Jobes, *Esther*, NIV Application Commentary (Zondervan, 1999), 94.
5. Anthony Tomasino, *Esther*, Evangelical Exegetical Commentary (Lexham, 2016), 176.
6. For more on this, see William F. Albright, "The Lachish Cosmetic Burner and Esther 2:12," in *Studies in the Book of Esther*, ed. Carey A. Moore (Ktav, 1982), 361–68.
7. Carl R. Anderson, study note for Esther 2:16–18 in *Holman Christian Standard Study Bible: God's Word for Life*, ed. Edwin A. Blum and Jeremy Royal Howard (Holman Bible Publishers, 2010).
8. John T. Bendor-Samuel, "Esther," in *International Bible Commentary with the New International Version*, ed. F. F. Bruce, H. L. Ellison, and G. C. D. Howley (Zondervan, 1979), 514.
9. Tomasino, *Esther*, 186.
10. Jobes, *Esther*, 103.
11. Sandra Glahn, *Espresso with Esther*, Coffee Cup Bible Studies (AMG, 2006), 3.

Lesson 3: Divine Providence Behind the Curtain

1. Mervin Breneman, *Ezra, Nehemiah, Esther*, New American Commentary, vol. 10 (B&H, 1993), 321.
2. Karen H. Jobes, *Esther*, NIV Application Commentary (Zondervan, 1999), 118.
3. Breneman, *Ezra, Nehemiah, Esther*, 323.
4. Timothy S. Laniak, "Esther," in *Ezra, Nehemiah, Esther*, ed. Leslie C. Allen and Timothy S. Laniak, Understanding the Bible Commentary Series (Baker Books, 2012), 143, ebook.
5. Jobes, *Esther*, 121.
6. Edwin M. Yamauchi, *Persia and the Bible* (Baker, 1990), 408.
7. Peter H. W. Lau, *Esther: A Pastoral and Contextual Commentary* (Langham, 2018), 42.
8. "Some Were Neighbors," United States Holocaust Memorial Museum, accessed June 18, 2025, https://www.ushmm.org/teach/teaching-materials/roles-of-individuals/ethical-leadership/some-were-neighbors.

Lesson 4: Divine Providence in the Turbulence

1. Karen H. Jobes, *Esther*, NIV Application Commentary (Zondervan, 1999), 131.
2. Anthony Tomasino, *Esther*, Evangelical Exegetical Commentary (Lexham, 2016), 238.
3. Tomasino, *Esther*, 243.
4. George Rawlinson and J. R. Thomson, "Esther," in *Pulpit Commentary*, ed. H. D. M. Spence and Joseph S. Exell, vol. 7, *Ezra, Nehemiah, Esther and Job* (Eerdmans, 1950), 83.
5. Julie A. Gorman, *Community That Is Christian: A Handbook on Small Groups* (Baker Books, 2002), 12.
6. Arthur W. Pink, *The Attributes of God*, 2nd ed. (Baker Books, 2006), 41.
7. John Bisagno, *God Is* (Victor, 1983), 11.

8. *Exploring Christian Scripture: Your Guide to the World of the Bible*, ed. Glenn R. Kreider et al. (B&H, 2024), 124.
9. Joyce G. Baldwin, *Esther: An Introduction and Commentary*, Tyndale Old Testament Commentaries (InterVarsity, 1984), 81.
10. Peter H. W. Lau, *Esther: A Pastoral and Contextual Commentary* (Langham, 2018), 52.
11. See the section "Korea Under Japanese Rule," in *Britannica*, "Korea," by Bae-ho Hahn and Ki-baik Lee, last updated January 24, 2025, https://www.britannica.com/place/Korea/Korea-under-Japanese-rule.
12. Beatrice Lăpădat, "Ahn Ei Sook: The Wolf Tamer," *ST Network*, June 12, 2023, https://st.network/analysis/top/ahn-ei-sook-the-wolf-tamer.html.

Lesson 5: Divine Providence in the Waiting

1. Karen H. Jobes, *Esther*, NIV Application Commentary (Zondervan, 1999), 144.
2. Gary V. Smith, *Ezra-Nehemiah and Esther*, Cornerstone Biblical Commentary 5b (Tyndale House, 2010), 260.
3. Smith, *Ezra-Nehemiah and Esther*, 261.
4. Charles R. Swindoll, *Esther: A Woman of Strength and Dignity* (Nelson, 1997), 101.
5. Swindoll, *Esther*, 97.
6. Matthew Henry, *Matthew Henry's Commentary on the Whole Bible: Complete and Unabridged in One Volume* (Hendrickson, 1994), 648.
7. C. S. Lewis, *Mere Christianity*, rev. ed. (HarperCollins, 2001), 124.
8. Eugene H. Peterson, *A Long Obedience in the Same Direction: Discipleship in an Instant Society* (InterVarsity, 2021), 37.

Lesson 6: Divine Providence Unfurled

1. H. A Ironside, *Ezra, Nehemiah, and Esther*, Ironside Expository Commentary (Kregel, 2008), 185.
2. Karen H. Jobes, *Esther*, NIV Application Commentary (Zondervan, 1999), 159.
3. Charles R. Swindoll, *Esther: A Woman of Strength and Dignity* (Nelson, 1997), 114.
4. Study note for Esther 6:10–13 in *NLT Chronological Life Application Study Bible*, 3rd ed. (Tyndale House, 2019).
5. Gary V. Smith, *Ezra-Nehemiah and Esther*, Cornerstone Biblical Commentary 5b (Tyndale House, 2010), 265.
6. Jobes, *Esther*, 152.
7. Gerald Cowen, "Pride," in *Holman Illustrated Bible Dictionary: The Complete Guide to Everything You Need to Know About the Bible*, ed. Chad Brand et al. (Holman Reference, 2003), 1327.
8. The Westminster Assembly, Westminster Confession of Faith, 3.1.
9. Jobes, *Esther*, 42.
10. Study note for Esther 6:7–9 in *NLT Chronological Life Application Study Bible*, 3rd ed. (Tyndale House, 2019).
11. Smith, *Ezra-Nehemiah and Esther*, 223.

12. Irving L. Jensen, *Ezra, Nehemiah, and Esther: A Self-Study Guide* (Moody, 1991), 95.
13. Jobes, *Esther,* 165.
14. Smith, *Ezra-Nehemiah and Esther,* 271.
15. Tony Evans, *The Tony Evans Bible Commentary: Advancing God's Kingdom Agenda* (Holman Reference, 2019), 35.

Lesson 7: Divine Providence Fulfilled

1. Josephus, *Antiquities* 11.17.
2. Timothy Cain, *The God of Great Reversals: The Gospel in the Book of Esther* (CreateSpace, 2016), 145.
3. Peter H. W. Lau, *Esther: A Pastoral and Contextual Commentary* (Langham, 2018), 42–43.
4. Irving L. Jensen, *Ezra, Nehemiah, and Esther: A Self-Study Guide* (Moody, 1991), 98.
5. Charles R. Swindoll, *Esther: A Woman of Strength and Dignity* (Nelson, 1997), x.
6. Karen H. Jobes and Janet Nygren, *Esther: God Fulfills a Promise,* Bringing the Bible to Life (Zondervan, 2008), 72.
7. Mervin Breneman, *Ezra, Nehemiah, Esther,* New American Commentary, vol. 10 (B&H, 1993), 353.
8. Swindoll, *Esther,* xii.
9. Adele Berlin, *Esther: The Traditional Hebrew Text with the New JPS Translation,* JPS Bible Commentary, vol. 17 (Jewish Publication Society, 2001), 72.
10. Karen H. Jobes, *Esther,* NIV Application Commentary (Zondervan, 1999), 86, 88.
11. Gary V. Smith, *Ezra-Nehemiah and Esther,* Cornerstone Biblical Commentary 5b (Tyndale House, 2010), 226.
12. Jobes, *Esther,* 211.
13. Smith, *Ezra-Nehemiah and Esther,* 226.
14. Swindoll, *Esther,* 17–18.
15. "It has been supposed that Jacob's object in conferring this distinction on Joseph was to mark him out as the heir to whom the forfeited birthright of Reuben (1 Ch. 5:1) was to be transferred." See Thomas Whitelaw, "Genesis," in *Pulpit Commentary,* ed. Henry D. M. Spence, vol. 1, *Genesis and Exodus* (Hendrickson, 1980), 427.

Lesson 8: Divine Providence Celebrated

1. John Bisagno, *God Is* (Victor, 1983), 11.
2. Charles R. Swindoll, *Esther: A Woman of Strength and Dignity* (Nelson, 1997), 158.
3. Swindoll, *Esther,* 165.
4. Gary V. Smith, *Ezra-Nehemiah and Esther,* Cornerstone Biblical Commentary 5b (Tyndale House, 2010), 279.
5. Karen H. Jobes, *Esther,* NIV Application Commentary (Zondervan, 1999), 196.
6. Josephus, *Antiquities* 11.291.
7. See Smith, *Ezra-Nehemiah and Esther,* 280.

8. Swindoll, *Esther*, 162.
9. Jobes, *Esther*, 202.
10. Irving L. Jensen, *Ezra, Nehemiah, and Esther: A Self-Study Guide* (Moody, 1991), 98.
11. Swindoll, *Esther*, 7.
12. Luci Swindoll, *You Bring the Confetti, God Brings the Joy* (Thomas Nelson, 2008), 13.
13. Jobes, *Esther*, 72.
14. Sources referenced in this section include Wade Goodwyn, "Charleston's Black Leaders Want to See Justice as Much as Forgiveness," *NPR*, July 2, 2015, https://www.npr.org/2015/07/02/419405863/charlestons-black-leaders-want-justice-as-much-as-forgiveness; Khushbu Shah and Eliott C. McLaughlin, "Victim's Dad Warns Dylann Roof: 'Your Creator . . . He's Coming for You," *CNN*, January 11, 2017, https://www.cnn.com/2017/01/11/us/dylann-roof-sentencing/; "'I Forgive You': Charleston Church Victims' Families Confront Suspect," *The Guardian*, June 19, 2015, https://www.theguardian.com/world/2015/jun/19/i-forgive-you-charleston-church-victims-families-confront-suspect; "After 54 Years, Confederate Flag Comes Down in S.C.," *CBS News*, July 10, 2015, https://www.cbsnews.com/news/confederate-flag-south-carolina-state house-grounds-comes-down/.
15. Smith, *Ezra-Nehemiah and Esther*, 217.
16. Dan Simmons Jr. as quoted in Khushbu Shah and Eliott C. McLaughlin, "Victim's Dad Warns Dylann Roof: 'Your Creator . . . He's Coming for You," *CNN*, January 11, 2017, https://www.cnn.com/2017/01/11/us/dylann-roof-sentencing/.
17. Anthony Thompson as quoted in "'I Forgive You': Charleston Church Victims' Families Confront Suspect," *The Guardian*, June 19, 2015, https://www.theguardian.com/world/2015/jun/19/i-forgive-you-charleston-church-victims-families-confront-suspect.
18. Catherine E. Shoichet and Khushbu Shah, "Dylann Roof Diary: 'I Do Not Regret What I Did. I Am Not Sorry,'" *CNN*, January 5, 2017, https://www.cnn.com/2017/01/05/us/dylann-roof-trial.
19. Alanna Simmons as quoted in "'I Forgive You': Charleston Church Victims' Families Confront Suspect," *The Guardian*, June 19, 2015, https://www.theguardian.com/world/2015/jun/19/i-forgive-you-charleston-church-victims-families-confront-suspect.

About the Authors

Sue Edwards is professor emeritus of educational ministries and leadership (her specialization is women's studies) at Dallas Theological Seminary (DTS), where she has had the opportunity to equip men and women for future ministry. She brings more than forty years of experience into the classroom as a Bible teacher, curriculum writer, and overseer of several megachurch women's ministries. As minister to women at Irving Bible Church and director of women's ministry at Prestonwood Baptist Church in Dallas, she has worked with women from all walks of life, ages, and stages. Her passion is to see modern and postmodern women connect, learn from one another, and bond around God's Word. Her Bible studies have ushered thousands of women—all over the country and overseas—into deeper Scripture study and community experiences.

With Kelley Mathews, Sue has coauthored *Organic Ministry to Women: A Guide to Transformational Ministry with Next Generation Women*, *Women's Retreats: A Creative Planning Guide*, and *Leading Women Who Wound: Strategies for an Effective Ministry*. Sue and Kelley joined with Henry J. Rogers to coauthor *Mixed Ministry: Working Together as Brothers and Sisters in an Oversexed Society*. *Organic Mentoring: A Mentor's Guide to Relationships with Next Generation Women*, coauthored with Barbara Neumann, explores the new values, preferences, and problems of the next generation and shows mentors how to avoid potential land mines and how to mentor successfully. She coedited *Invitation to Educational Ministry: Foundations of Transformative Christian Education* with the DTS vice president for education and professor of educational ministries and leadership, George M. Hillman Jr. The book serves as a primary academic textbook for schools all over the country as well as a handbook for church leaders. She also contributed two chapters to *Instructional Strategies for Christian Teachers: How to Teach the Bible and Theology in the Church and School* by James Riley Estep Jr. and Jay L. Sedwick.

Sue's latest book with Mathews, *40 Questions About Women in Ministry*, has received two prestigious distinctions: the Editor's Choice Award from the Christian Editors Association and a finalist position for the ECPA Christian Book Award in the category of Ministry Resources. She is also the author of nineteen Bible studies in her Discover Together Bible Study series.

Sue earned a doctor of ministry degree from Gordon–Conwell Theological Seminary in Boston, a master's in Bible from DTS, and a bachelor's in journalism from Trinity University.

Married for fifty-four years, she and David are the proud parents of two married daughters and the grandparents of five. David is a retired computer engineer who serves the Lord as a lay prison chaplain. Sue loves chocolate, strong decaf coffee, and taking walks with their Westies, Quigley and Itsy Bitsy Mitzi.

Rebecca Carrell is, in order of importance, a joyful Jesus follower, wife to Mike, mother to Caitlyn and Nick, Bible teacher, conference speaker, author, and award-winning broadcaster. After spending over twenty years as a morning radio host in Dallas–Fort Worth, she now serves as an adjunct professor at Dallas Theological Seminary (DTS) in the media arts & worship and educational ministries & leadership departments as she works toward her doctor of education degree.

One of Rebecca's great passions is helping Christians understand the metanarrative of the Bible, and she travels nationally and internationally to teach the *Story of Scripture* with DTS President Dr. Mark Yarbrough and Vice President of Communications Dr. Josh Winn. The three host the *What Does the Bible Say?* podcast, which examines current issues through a biblical lens. She also leads women's retreats and events at churches across the United States.

Rebecca hosts and produces the podcast *Honestly, Though: Real Talk. Real Life. Real Faith.* Her books include *Holy Jellybeans: Finding God Through Everyday Things*; *Holy Hiking Boots: When God Makes the Ordinary Extraordinary*; and *Anxious for Nothing: Paul's Letter to the Philippians.* She recently joined Dr. Sue Edwards as a coauthor of the Discover Together Bible Study series for studies on 1 Timothy, Hebrews, and Esther.

Connect with Rebecca on X (formerly known as Twitter), Instagram, and Facebook, or through www.rebeccacarrell.com.